Bruce Byfield

Character and Paragraph Styles

Designing with LibreOffice, Extract 3

Editor & Publisher

Jean Hollis Weber, Friends of OpenDocument, Inc., 544 Carlyle Gardens, Beck Drive North, Condon, Queensland 4815, Australia. Please direct any comments or suggestions about this document to info@friendsofopendocument.com.

Reviewers

Jean Hollis Weber, Lee Schlesinger, Nicola Einarson, Terry Hancock, Charlie Kravetz, Michael Manning, Jean-Francois Nifenecker, Georges Rodier, Christina Teskey.

Special thanks also go to Marcel Gagné, Michael Meeks, and Carla Schroder for advanced reading.

Acknowledgments

Parts of this book's content were originally published, sometimes in different forms, by Linux Journal, Linux.com, Linux Pro Magazine, Open Content and Software, Wazi, and WorldLabel. My thanks for permission to re-use this material.

Publication date and software version

Published October 2018. Based on LibreOffice Version 5.0.2.2 and later.

Photo credits

Cover photos and the photo on the interior title page are copyright by Bruce Byfield and released under the Creative Commons Attribution Sharealike License, version 3.0 or later.

They depict the Sun Yat Sen Classical Garden in Vancouver, Canada. The gardens are based on the philosophy of feng shui, which, like typography, works deliberately to produce a natural, unnoticed effect. All photos are used with permission.

Table of Contents

Chapter 1

Chapter 2

Chapter 3

Chapter 4

For Trish, Always

1

Introduction

This book is an extract from a much larger book entitled *Designing with LibreOffice*. It is intended for those who only want information on designing and using character and paragraph styles in LibreOffice, the popular free-licensed office suite. It consists of Chapter 5, 6 and 7 from the larger book.

This book will eventually become the third of five excerpts from the complete book.

The excerpts will be:

Part 1: Styles and Templates (already released)
Part 2: Choosing Fonts (already released)
Part 3: Character and Paragraph Styles
Part 4: Page, Frame, and List Styles
Part 5: Slide Shows, Diagrams, and Spreadsheets

The emphasis in each book is design. In all of them, design is defined, not as formatting that calls attention to itself, like an HTML blink tag, but as formatting that is attractive and makes a document easy to read, edit, and maintain.

Together, the five smaller books will contain most, but not all the information from the larger book. Any changes are minimal, and made for continuity or changes in structure made necessary by the changes in format.

Tip

You can download the entire *Designing with LibreOffice* book or (when available) other excerpts from:

http://designingwithlibreoffice.com/download-buy/

Printed versions of the entire book or of excerpts are available for sale at the Friends of Open Document store at:

http://www.lulu.com/spotlight/opendocument

If you need information on features or selections that are not mentioned in this book, see the LibreOffice documentation page:

https://documentation.libreoffice.org/en/english-documentation/

Printed versions of the LibreOffice manuals are available for sale at the Friends of Open Document store at:

http://www.lulu.com/spotlight/opendocument

2

Spacing on all sides

Paragraph styles are the most frequently used type of style in LibreOffice. However, they interact so closely with character styles that talking about one without the other is impossible – they even share several of the same tabs in their dialog windows.

Paragraph styles define the general formatting for any text-heavy document, while character styles provide brief variations. For short bursts of text – for example, a title, URL, or bullet point – character styles provide exceptions that give paragraph styles the flexibility they lack by themselves.

The excerpt *Choosing Fonts* ventures into some of the basics of paragraph and character settings while discussing fonts and how to find the ideal line spacing. This chapter expands upon and completes the discussion of basic paragraph formatting, (including a more detailed discussion of line spacing), covering the options for vertical and horizontal spacing.

The next two chapters discuss special features and potential problems and advanced features.

Tip

Many of the tabs in character and paragraph style dialog windows reappear in the other LibreOffice applications.

Preparing to design

- Choose your fonts and ideal line spacing.

- Have a calculator and a list of multiples of the line spacing ready so you can check basic measurements.

- Set the default measurement unit to points in TOOLS > OPTIONS > LIBREOFFICE WRITER > GENERAL > SETTINGS > MEASUREMENT UNIT. You can reset the default unit to centimeters or inches when you are done, but points are the most commonly used unit of measurement for general typography.

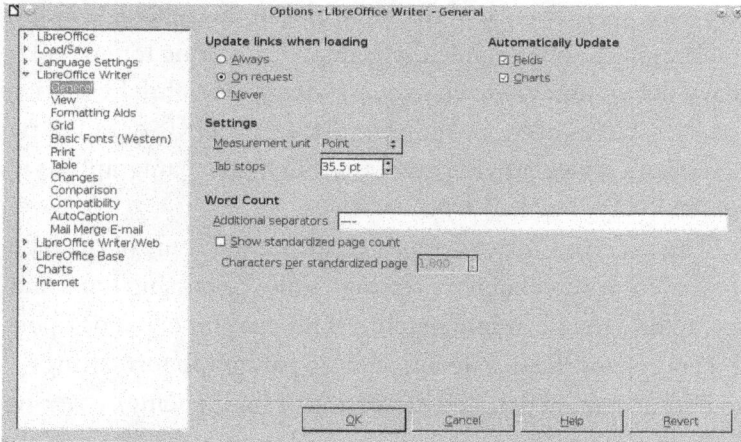

Before you design, set the MEASUREMENT UNIT to points.

- Set the zoom to 100% so you can judge the page color. Print or zoom in or out periodically so you can get a different perspective.

- In the status bar at the bottom of the editing window, set LibreOffice to display multiple pages, selecting the third button from the left. Unless you are struggling with a small monitor, a two-page spread helps you see the effect of your design choices.

Displaying multiple pages shows how the document will look when printed or else viewed on a wide screen monitor in a two-page spread.

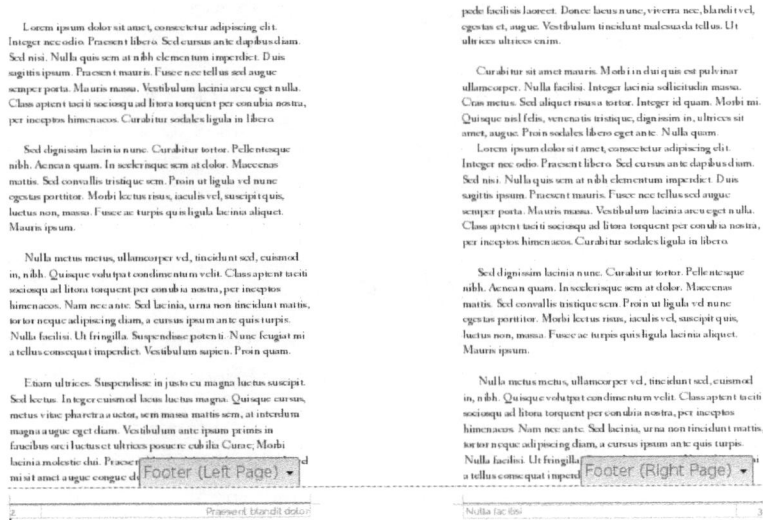

A multi-page display gives a design overview. Here, it confirms that footers are mirrored as intended.

- Open a second file where you can experiment and use dummy text to test formats.

- While you design, use manual formatting. Creating styles at this point is just an extra step until you have finished experimenting. When you have decided on the formatting choices, you can always drag a selected passage to the STYLES AND FORMATTING window to create a style from it.

- Use this chapter's headings as a checklist so you cover all the basic formatting.

STOP

Caution

As you work, you may find that some of the settings you have already chosen require changing – even the magic number.

Rather than resisting the change, accept it as a natural part of the design process. The goal is to develop the best design you can, not to cling to a pointless consistency.

Planning text styles

You can save time while designing by working whenever possible with Writer's pre-defined styles. Later, as you write, you will find that some features, such as INSERT > FIELDS > OTHER DOCUMENT > CHAPTER > CHAPTER NAME field, depend on the pre-defined paragraph styles being in the document.

The pre-defined character and paragraph styles should cover most of your needs, but you can add other styles as needed.

Then go through the list of pre-defined styles and decide which ones you do not need. For example, paragraph styles

HEADING 5–10 are far more headings than anyone can manage. Perhaps, too, you have no use for paragraph styles like LIST 1 CONT., LIST 1 END, and LIST 1 START, and they will only clutter up the STYLES AND FORMATTING window. For each unnecessary style, select HIDE from the right-click menu. Should you decide that you need a hidden style after all, you can go to the HIDDEN STYLES view and select SHOW instead.

All these tasks are a lot of work. But you will also find that there are many styles in which you can keep the default settings.

For instance, line spacing may be unimportant in headings, since headings are often less than a single line in length.

Similarly, in a simple document, an automatic first line indent may completely remove the need to set tab stops. The fact that many defaults can be used unchanged or entirely ignored greatly reduces the amount of designing necessary to complete a template.

Setting vertical line spacing

Writer's LINE SPACING field is on the INDENTS AND SPACING tab of each paragraph style. It used to accept entries of 1/10 of a point (1/720 of an inch), but, since LibreOffice 4.2, the field rounds entries to the nearest point (1/72 of an inch).

This rounding produces adequate results, but not always optimal ones. Believe it or not, 1/10 of a point can make a large visual difference.

Tip

Apache OpenOffice still allows entries of 1/10 points.

If you used your choice of fonts to determine the magic number, as explained in *Choosing Fonts,* then you have already adjusted this option using the FIXED setting in the LINE SPACING field. FIXED remains by far the best setting, because it is the only option that gives an exact measurement.

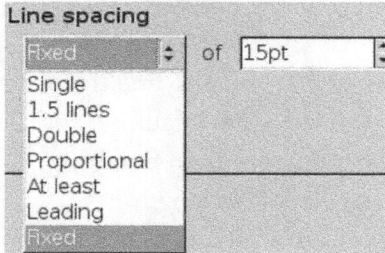

Line spacing options for paragraphs.

FIXED also has the advantage that documents will be register-true, regardless of whether the REGISTER-TRUE setting is turned on. In other words, lines will be in the same horizontal position on all pages, especially if the document uses only one font.

In addition, should you print on both sides of a page, the lines will overlap in most places, preventing the shadow of the other page showing through thin paper.

However, one problem with paragraph styles with larger font sizes, such as headings, is that they can have the tops or bottoms of letters cut off when FIXED is used. This problem can be solved by setting the LINE SPACING field using the AT LEAST option while keeping the line height unchanged.

Line-spacing problem with fixed setting

Cut-off characters are a sign that the FIXED line spacing needs to be either adjusted or replaced by AT LEAST.

The other options for line spacing are different ways of expressing line spacing. Except for quick, one-off documents, avoid the SINGLE, 1.5 LINES, and DOUBLE options. These options use Writer's standard defaults for line spacing, and are optimal for any given font only by luck.

The least useful option is PROPORTIONAL, in which line-spacing is expressed as a percentage of the automatically determined single space, and not an exact figure. In other words, this option places you two removes from the actual figure for line spacing.

Another vague option is LEADING. "Leading" is a term from the days of manual typesetting, when scraps of lead or anything else around the print shop were used to increase line spacing. "Leading" came to refer to the entire line spacing. However, LibreOffice uses the word to refer to only the extra space beyond the font size. For example, in LibreOffice, a paragraph set to 12/15 would be set with LEADING at 3 points.

Line spacing at small font sizes

You can sometimes find fonts specially designed to be readable at sizes below 10 points. More often, small font sizes need extra line spacing to make them readable.

Unfortunately, LibreOffice, like most word processors, treats line spacing for small font sizes the same as line spacing for any other size. As a rule, select FIXED to give small font sizes the extra line spacing they need.

Lorem ipsum dolor sit amet, consectetur adipiscing elit. Donec a diam lectus. Sed sit amet ipsum mauris. Maecenas congue ligula ac quam viverra nec consectetur ante hendrerit. Donec et mollis dolor. Praesent et diam eget libero egestas mattis sit amet vitae augue. Nam tincidunt congue enim, ut porta lorem lacinia consectetur. Donec ut libero sed arcu vehicula ultricies a non tortor. Lorem ipsum dolor sit amet, consectetur adipiscing elit. Aenean ut

Lorem ipsum dolor sit amet, consectetur adipiscing elit. Donec a diam lectus. Sed sit amet ipsum mauris. Maecenas congue ligula ac quam viverra nec consectetur ante hendrerit. Donec et mollis dolor. Praesent et diam eget libero egestas mattis sit amet vitae augue. Nam tincidunt congue enim, ut porta lorem lacinia consectetur. Donec ut libero sed arcu vehicula ultricies a non tortor. Lorem ipsum dolor sit amet, consectetur adipiscing elit. Aenean ut

Above: 8 point Liberation Serif with automatic single spacing. Below: 8/12 Liberation Serif. Font sizes of less than 10 points almost always require extra line-spacing for readability.

Spacing between paragraphs

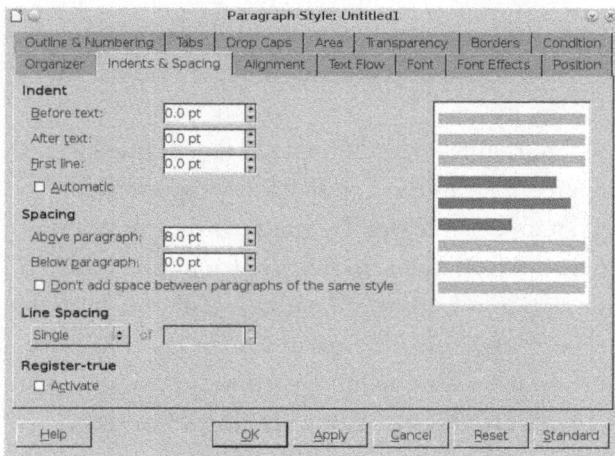

The INDENTS & SPACING tab, with the ABOVE PARAGRAPH and BELOW PARAGRAPH fields listed under SPACING.

Vertical spacing is set on the INDENTS AND SPACING tab in the SPACING > ABOVE PARAGRAPH and SPACING > BELOW PARAGRAPH.

Vertical spacing is also used to increase the effectiveness of headings. The rule is simple: Put a heading closer to the content it summarizes, and the relation between the heading and the content becomes clear at a glance.

vitae at nunc. Ut est nunc, malesuada nec ante sed, ullamcorper placerat orci. Duis volutpat dui at erat posuere fringilla. Duis interdum consectetur nisl porttitor pellentesque. Fusce tincidunt felis non nulla commodo varius. Nam dolor diam, laoreet blandit suscipit nec, lacinia eget nisi.

Vivamus sit amet convallis velit,

Nullam semper eu leo quis pulvinar. Morbi id consectetur nunc. Cras sollicitudin vehicula tellus quis feugiat. Cras vulputate arcu ac lorem placerat, sit amet dignissim erat ornare. Praesent eleifend pharetra sagittis. Ut turpis diam, sodales sit amet dolor lobortis, ultricies aliquet magna. Nulla libero dui,

Putting less space between headings and the passage they introduce helps the eye to associate them.

Extra spacing between paragraphs is one of the ways to indicate the start of a new paragraph (the other is an indentation of the first line). Usually, extra spacing is used in technical documents, but the only rule is not to use both at the same time.

Tip

The heading's font size, and the space above and below it, should total a multiple of the line spacing. In this way, heading paragraph styles match the line spacing every few lines.

Use the same formula if spacing between body text paragraphs is used instead of a first line indentation.

> nulla commodo varius. Nam dolor diam, laoreet blandit suscipit nec, lacinia eget nisi.

[15 pts]

[16 pts] Vivamus sit amet convallis velit
[6.5 pts]

> Nullam semper eu leo quis pulvinar. Morbi id consectetur nunc. Cras sollicitudin vehicula

37.5 pts = 15 x 2.5

In this example, the line spacing is set to 15 points. Together, the spacing before the heading and after it plus the font size for the heading should equal a multiple of 15 or of 7.5 (half the line height).

Removing unexpected space

The combined effect of BEFORE and AFTER settings for two subsequent paragraph styles can cause unexpectedly large spaces between paragraphs.

Minimize this problem by using only the BEFORE PARAGRAPH field and leaving the AFTER PARAGRAPH field set to zero for most paragraph styles.

In the case of pictures, you may want to vary the spacing to avoid extra large gaps.

Sometimes, the conflict may be between an image and a paragraph style. When that happens, modify the space below the image so that it matches the convention you have set and leave the paragraph style settings alone. After all, spacing around an image or any other object is manually set already.

Avoiding widows and orphans

Standard typography tries to avoid a single line at the bottom of a page – an orphan – or a single line at the top of a page – a widow.

Tip

You can distinguish widows from orphans by remembering that an orphan is left behind while a widow goes forward by herself.

Of course, avoiding widows and orphans is not always possible. Some paragraphs are a single line long. TOOLS > AUTOCORRECT does have an option to combine short paragraphs, but that is not always suitable to the sense of the passage.

Other paragraphs have a number of lines that do not fit Writer's settings. For example, if you have set last and first paragraphs on a page to each have two lines, something has to give when a three-line paragraph straddles two pages.

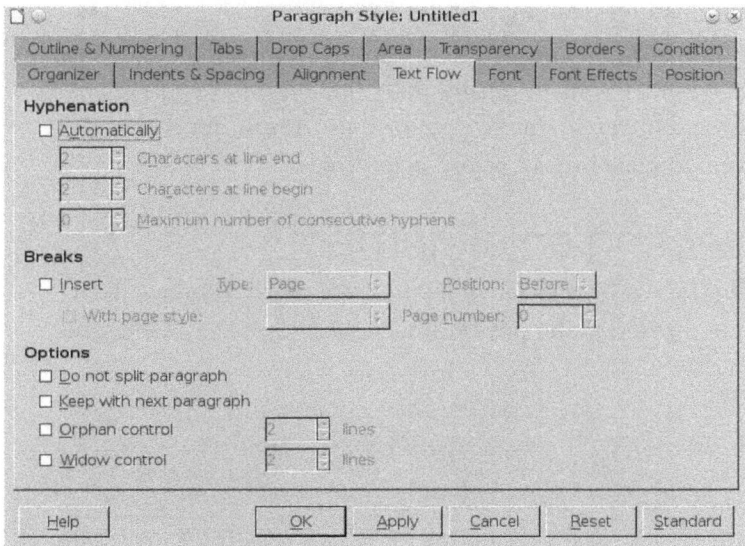

The TEXT FLOW tab, with ORPHAN CONTROL and WIDOW CONTROL under OPTIONS.

The TEXT FLOW tab of a paragraph style includes four options for avoiding both.

The main tools for avoiding widows and orphans are WIDOW CONTROL and ORPHAN CONTROL. For TEXT BODY and related styles, you should activate both, accepting the default of keeping two lines together, or three at the most. You do not need these settings for heading paragraphs, or in a case in which all paragraphs are short – in either case, the controls will have nothing to adjust.

As an alternative, keep WIDOW CONTROL and ORPHAN CONTROL unselected and select instead DO NOT SPLIT PARAGRAPH. This setting may keep important information together and therefore easier to read, but can result in page breaks well before the bottom of the page.

For headings, you may prefer KEEP WITH NEXT PARAGRAPH. When headings are meant to introduce the body text below them, having the heading and body text on separate pages makes no sense. However, this setting, too, may result in poorly positioned page breaks, so use it sparingly.

Selecting an alignment

On the ALIGNMENT tab of a paragraph style, you have four choices for horizontal positioning: LEFT, RIGHT, CENTERED, and JUSTIFIED.

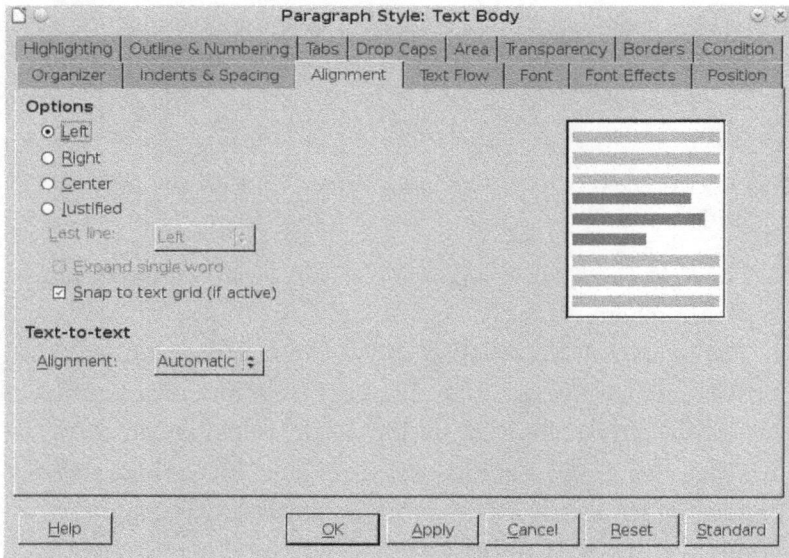

The ALIGNMENT tab, with the OPTIONS at the top of the window.

RIGHT is rarely used except in short, highly-formatted documents such as ads or diagrams, while CENTERED is generally reserved for titles and sub-titles. For most paragraph styles, your choice is likely to be LEFT or JUSTIFIED.

Whatever your choice of alignment, if you are using hyphenated styles, run TOOLS > LANGUAGE > HYPHENATION as a last step before publishing. This selection repairs any sub-optimal choices Writer might have made on the fly.

Using a Justified alignment

Many users prefer a Justified alignment, in which all lines start at the same position on the left and end at the same position on the right. Because commercial publications often use Justified, users often believe it looks more professional.

The preference may also be a reminder of the earliest days of word processing, the first time that a Justified alignment became practical. The vast majority of typewriters, of course, could only use a Left alignment.

The trouble is, a Justified alignment often requires more work. Too often, it results in irregular spacing between characters or words that looks far worse than Left alignment ever could. You almost always need to tinker to find the best distribution of characters and words on a line.

Generally, too, the shorter line, the harder you have to work to make Justified work. As a rule, lines of less than 40 characters are too much effort to be worth justifying. A Left alignment can still cause problems, but they are often less severe, especially in columns or tables.

The easiest way to tell if a paragraph style can easily use Justified is to set it up with dummy text and count the number of lines that end in a hyphen and the blotches of irregular white space.

The more of these problems that appear, the more you need to change the hyphenation, the font, the font size, and/or the column width in the hope of a better fit. You can even go to the POSITION tab to expand or condense character spacing.

Lorem ip-	suere vitae,	tor elit id
sum dolor	molestie in	tempus dic-
sit amet,	mauris.	tum. Donec
consectetur	Nunc ac-	tempus
adipiscing	cumsan	eleifend
elit. Etiam	ante a	porta. Nam
mauris dui,	lorem port-	elementum
pellen-	titor pulv-	venenatis
tesque sit	inar. Ae-	nisi id ali-
amet po-	nean portti-	quet. Nunc

An example of the wrong alignment for the line length. The middle column has three hyphenated lines, while hyphenation causes awkward breaks throughout. Even worse, several lines are single words. Some lines even have more than one fault.

Note

If you do decide to use full justification, you can tweak the result using Tools > Language > Hyphenation to manually adjust line by line where hyphenation occurs. However, this is such a painstaking task that it is usually only practical for either short or extremely important documents.

Setting the last line of justified text

The last line of justified text is only a complete line by luck. Almost always, it is an incomplete line.

LibreOffice offers several choices of how to handle this approach. Frankly, though, you have to wonder why. All but one leave large gaps between words or letters that anyone who cares about the design of their documents should find unacceptable.

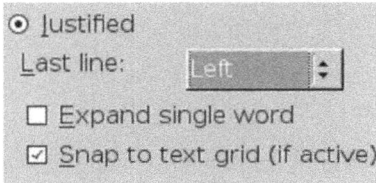

The LAST LINE options for justified text on the ALIGNMENT tab. The other options in the drop-down list are CENTERED and JUSTIFIED.

Tip

SNAP TO TEXT GRID (IF ACTIVE) uses the non-printing grid set in TOOLS > OPTIONS > LIBREOFFICE WRITER > GRID for positioning. Apache OpenOffice lacks this option.

The only consistently aesthetic choice is to set the LAST LINE field to LEFT. This selection is the only one that eliminates the impossible situation of trying to justify a line of text that is too short and has ugly gaps in it.

The other options – JUSTIFIED, CENTERED, EXPAND SINGLE WORD, and LEFT – all look awkward. The only reason to use any of them is to provide a sample of why they are unacceptable or in the unlikely case that you want to reproduce the look of a hastily typeset book or newspaper.

Lorem ipsum dolor sit amet, consectetur adipiscing elit. Integer nec odio. Praesent libero. Sed cursus ante dapibus diam. Sed nisi. Nulla quis sem at nibh elementum imperdiet. Duis sagittis ipsum. Praesent mauris. Fusce nec tellus sed augue semper porta. Mauris massa. Vestibulum lacinia arcu eget nulla. Class aptent

Lorem ipsum dolor sit amet, consectetur adipiscing elit. Integer nec odio. Praesent libero. Sed cursus ante dapibus diam. Sed nisi. Nulla quis sem at nibh elementum imperdiet. Duis sagittis ipsum. Praesent mauris. Fusce nec tellus sed augue semper porta. Mauris massa. Vestibulum lacinia arcu eget nulla. Class aptent

Lorem ipsum dolor sit amet, consectetur adipiscing elit. Integer nec odio. Praesent libero. Sed cursus ante dapibus diam. Sed nisi. Nulla quis sem at nibh elementum imperdiet. Duis sagittis ipsum. Praesent mauris. Fusce nec tellus sed augue semper porta
M   a   u   r   i   s

Lorem ipsum dolor sit amet, consectetur adipiscing elit. Integer nec odio. Praesent libero. Sed cursus ante dapibus diam. Sed nisi. Nulla quis sem at nibh elementum imperdiet. Duis sagittis ipsum. Praesent mauris. Fusce nec tellus sed augue semper porta. Mauris massa. Vestibulum lacinia arcu eget nulla. Class aptent

The justification of the last line. From top to bottom: JUSTIFIED, CENTERED, EXPAND SINGLE WORD, and LEFT.

You may be able to improve the look of JUSTIFIED by selecting SNAP TO TEXT GRID (IF ACTIVE) and adjusting the grid set in TOOLS > OPTIONS > LIBREOFFICE WRITER > GRID. However, getting an acceptable look is likely to take a lot of trial and error.

Using a Left alignment

When a paragraph has a Left alignment, all lines start at the same position on the left, but can end anywhere on the right. For this reason, a Left alignment is sometimes referred to as "ragged right." This is the default choice in Writer, probably because it is reasonably acceptable without tweaking, especially if lines are not hyphenated or are over about 40 characters long.

Generally, the shorter the line, the harder you have to work to make Justified look decent. That means that Left can be a better choice in columns or tables.

Setting hyphenation

Hyphenation options are set on the TEXT FLOW tab. Whether to hyphenate is one of the most important design decisions you will make when designing a document.

Hyphenation is a contentious issue in digital design. Most word processors hyphenate as you type, and while they make adjustments as the line lengths change, their on-the-fly solutions are not always optional. Short lines are especially hard to hyphenate well automatically.

These difficulties are one reason that many designers prefer a Left alignment or ragged right margin. A Left alignment does not always produce the best possible use of the line, but its shortcomings are rarely as severe as those with a Justified alignment.

Another choice is to turn off hyphenation completely, which is probably why the TEXT FLOW tab does not check the AUTOMATICALLY hyphenation box by default.

Other designers, more determined or more patient, try to improve hyphenation by adjusting the settings on the TEXT FLOW tab. The number of letters at the end and start of the line should be 1–4. The typographical convention is not to allow more than two lines in a row to end with a hyphen.

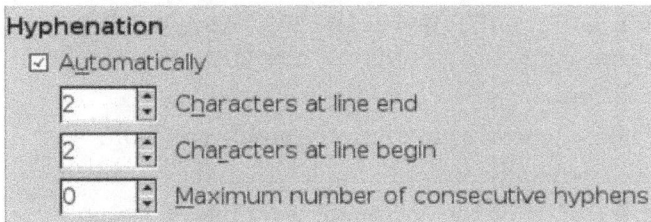

Detail of the TEXT FLOW tab, showing the hyphenation controls.

The CHARACTERS AT LINE END and CHARACTERS AT LINE BEGIN fields can sometimes be manipulated to improve hyphenation by playing one off against the other. Working by itself, the MAXIMUM NUMBER OF CONSECUTIVE HYPHENS field can also make a difference.

In many documents, only TEXT BODY and perhaps another handful of paragraph styles are used at such length that hyphenation can improve how they fall on the page. Headings, which are rarely more than a few words long and almost never more than two lines, generally do not need to be hyphenated at all. If anything, headings are easier to scan if not hyphenated.

You may want to change the hyphenation by adjusting:

- The HYPHENATION settings on the TEXT FLOW tab.

- The font weight or size.

- The choice of fonts.

- The settings for TOOLS > OPTIONS > LANGUAGE SETTINGS > WRITING AIDS > OPTIONS > MINIMAL NUMBER OF CHARACTERS FOR HYPHENATION. These settings are over-ridden by any formatting in the document itself.

- The SCALE WIDTH and SPACING fields on the POSITION tab to expand or condense character spacing. Frankly, these fields are a last desperate measure.

In addition, if you do hyphenate, the line divisions can be improved by running TOOLS > LANGUAGE > HYPHENATION as a final touch on the document.

This tool not only works interactively, giving you more control, but also generally does a better job than the on-the-fly hyphenation, if run when the document is complete.

Tip

For extra fine-tuning, go through a document when it is complete, and hand-hyphenate by positioning the cursor between syllables and pressing CTRL+ -. This key combination creates a conditional hyphen that only

Character and Paragraph Styles

comes into play when it is in the hyphenation zone near the right margin.

Setting horizontal spacing

By default, paragraphs run from the left margin to the right margin – or, at least, to a region just before the right margin that LibreOffice must reach before starting a new line, with or without hyphenation.

However, on the INDENTS AND SPACING tab, you can indent a paragraph on the left by entering a value in the BEFORE TEXT field, or on the right by entering a value in the AFTER TEXT field.

Common uses for an indent include:

- The start of a new paragraph.

- A quotation of over three lines or 100 words. Typically, such long quotations are indented one line-space on the left and right. No quotation marks are used, since the indentation is enough to mark is a quotation.

- The space between a bullet or number and an item in a list. This space is set using the INDENT AT field on the POSITION tab for a list style.

- Notes, tips, or warning paragraph styles.

- Paragraph styles intended for single style outline numbering.

- Cases in which headers and footers are wider than body text.

Controlling the number of indents

Some paragraph styles that begin with an indentation are unavoidable in a text document. However, too many different indentations clutter the design, so indentations should be kept to a minimum. No need, for example, exists to have a bulleted or numbered list indented more than the TEXT BODY style. Instead, the indentation for a long quotation can be the same as the first line indentation, as well as the position where the text starts in a list item after a bullet or number.

Tip

Horizontal line spacing can also be a help in readability. Regardless of font or page size, typographic convention suggests that a line of body text should be 50–75 characters long for readability – or, to put things another way, two to three lower case alphabets long in a single-column layout.

In tables or multi-column layouts, the length should generally be 30–50 characters, regardless of alignment. Anything less risks cluttering the column with hyphens, single-word lines, and/or vast stretches of white space.

Lorem ipsum dolor sit amet, consectetur adipiscing elit. Donec a diam lectus. Sed sit amet ipsum mauris. Maecenas congue ligula ac quam viverra nec consectetur ante hendrerit. Donec et mollis dolor.
- Nam tincidunt congue enim, ut porta lorem lacinia consectetur.
- Donec ut libero sed arcu vehicula ultricies a non tortor.
- Lorem ipsum dolor sit amet, consectetur adipiscing elit.
  - Aenean ut gravida lorem.
  - Ut turpis felis, pulvinar a semper sed, adipiscing id dolor.
  - Pellentesque auctor nisi id magna consequat sagittis.

Lorem ipsum dolor sit amet, consectetur adipiscing elit. Donec a diam lectus. Sed sit amet ipsum mauris. Maecenas congue ligula ac quam viverra nec consectetur ante hendrerit. Donec et mollis dolor.
- Nam tincidunt congue enim, ut porta lorem lacinia consectetur.
- Donec ut libero sed arcu vehicula ultricies a non tortor.
- Lorem ipsum dolor sit amet, consectetur adipiscing elit.
  - Aenean ut gravida lorem.
  - Ut turpis felis, pulvinar a semper sed, adipiscing id dolor.
  - Pellentesque auctor nisi id magna consequat sagittis.

An example of why indents should be as few as possible. Starting at the left margin, the top passage has five indentations, and looks cluttered. The bottom passage looks less cluttered because it reduces the number of indentations to three.

Setting first line indentation

A first-line indent is one of the two ways to indicate a new paragraph. The other way is to add extra space between paragraphs.

Usually, a first-line indent is used for more formal or literary works, while an extra space may be for technical manuals, but the rule is not absolute. The only firm convention is that you should use one, not both at the same time, the way that many people seem do automatically. The advantage of a first line indent is that it saves paper.

Most people set an indent of 30–36 points (about half an inch) – no doubt a legacy of typewriters, on which setting indentations precisely was difficult. However, that is excessive at the 10–14 point font sizes used for most body text, where it looks awkward and unprofessional.

Unless a font is extremely small, the first line indent usually needs to be no more than the line spacing, and you might even manage with half a line-space, depending on the font size. Expeiment to see what is suitable in each case.

If you set the FIRST LINE field to AUTOMATIC, you can largely ignore tabs, except for features like tables of contents that rely upon them for some features. More importantly, after you have finished designing, you have no need to think about indentation while you work.

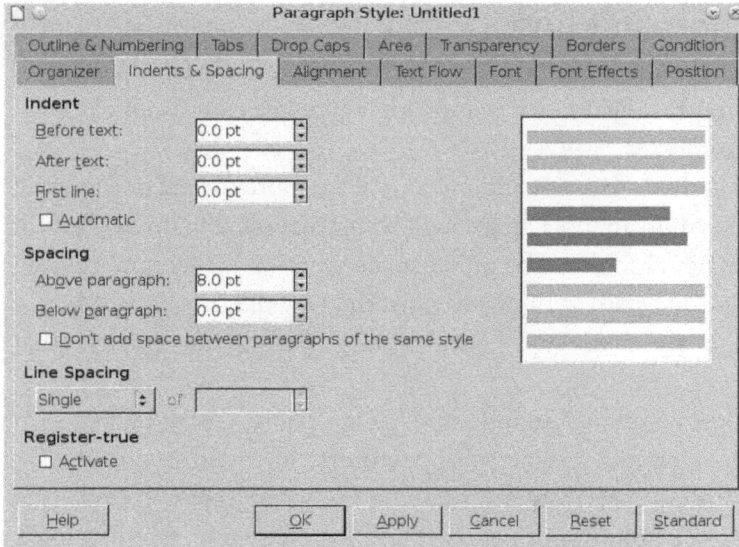

The first line indent is set in the FIRST LINE field of the INDENT section of the INDENTS & SPACING tab. You can use it either by pressing the TAB key or by selecting the AUTOMATIC box.

    Lorem ipsum dolor sit amet, consectetuer adipiscing elit, sed diam nonummy nibh

  Lorem ipsum dolor sit amet, consectetuer adipiscing elit, sed diam nonummy nibh

  Lorem ipsum dolor sit amet, consectetuer adipiscing elit, sed diam nonummy nibh

First line indentation. 36 points (top) can leave too much white space to the left, while half a line-space (bottom) can be hard to distinguish. Usually, a full line-space (middle) avoids both extremes.

Character and Paragraph Styles

Example: Designing a letter template

At this point, you may want a sense of what goes into a template.

You can customize a letter template from FILE > WIZARDS > LETTER that uses frames to position different elements of the letter. However, this template is more elaborate than it needs to be.

As a simpler alternative, here are the steps in building a letter template with styles rather than fields.

The example ignores page settings, since they have not been covered in this excerpt. For now, you can use the default settings, or adjust margins and headers to suit.

Choosing fonts

This template uses two fonts: One for the body of the letter, and one for information like addresses and the salutation – the equivalents of headers in other documents. Although it could just as easily use a single font, using a second one helps to differentiate the different parts of the letter.

After some experimentation, I opted for two free-licensed fonts from the Arkandis Digital Foundry. Baskervald ADF Std. imitates the classic Eighteenth Century font Baskerville and is used for body text. Gillius ADF No.2, which imitates Gill Sans, is used for heading text (that is, anything not part of the body text).

If you download and install these two fonts on your system, you can build the template by following the description below.

Creating the basic font palette

To prepare Gillius ADF No.2, apply these settings to the HEADING paragraph style:

- Since this font is only for short lines, ignore elements such as first line indentation or widow and orphan control, which will not be used.

- Set the font size to 14 points for greater legibility on the FONT tab, and set the line space to 18 points. Experiments with page color show that anything less makes the color of the font too dark on the page.

To prepare Baskervald ADF Std, apply these settings to the TEXT BODY style:

- Select the AUTOMATICALLY box for hyphenation, ORPHAN CONTROL, and WIDOW CONTROL on the TEXT FLOW tab.

- Set the font size to 15 on the FONT tab. Baskervald's characters use more white space than most fonts, and therefore appear much smaller than the actual size.

- Set the LINE SPACING to FIXED > 18 POINTS on the INDENTS & SPACING tab. This setting gives Baskervald a color close to that of Gillius, which makes for a uniform look on the page.

Check these settings by printing samples of at least three lines for both fonts. All other styles will be based on the settings for these two, with variations for individual needs.

Setting up other styles

The best way to set up other styles is to start at the top of the document and note the styles that are needed:

- Use the pre-existing ADDRESSEE style for the return address. Change the INHERIT FROM field on the ORGANIZER tab from ADDRESSEE to HEADER, and change the alignment to RIGHT on the ALIGNMENT tab.

STOP Caution

You may need to re-start LibreOffice for the changes to take effect. This problem may happen with any pre-existing style.

- Below the return address is the DATE style, which is followed by white space, then the ADDRESS. Create both as new styles linked to the HEADER style.

Then make the following changes to the DATE style:

1   Set the NEXT STYLE field on the ORGANIZER tab to ADDRESS.

2   Change the alignment to RIGHT on the ALIGNMENT tab.

3   On the INDENTS AND SPACING tab, set SPACING > ABOVE PARAGRAPH to 54 points, and SPACING > BELOW to 126 points. Notice that these are multiples of the fixed line spacing of 18 points being used for Header and its subordinate style.

Tip

If you are using any page size other than Letter, increase SPACING > BELOW to a multiple of 18.

4   From the menu, select INSERT > FIELDS > OTHER > DOCUMENT > DATE. Select a format from the FORMAT pane, then click the

INSERT button. Now, every time you select the DATE style, the current date will be automatically added.

5   The ADDRESS style is unmodified from the HEADER style. However, it is worth creating so you remember what style to use. Besides, you might eventually decide to modify it.

6   The next style is the SALUTATION. On the INDENTS & SPACING TAB, set SPACING > ABOVE PARAGRAPH to 36 points (2 lines), and SPACING > BELOW PARAGRAPH to 18 (1 line). Then, on the ORGANIZER tab, set the NEXT STYLE field to TEXT BODY.

7   The TEXT BODY style is already created. However, it needs a FIRST LINE INDENT setting on the INDENTS & SPACING tab. Set it to 18 points, the same as the line spacing.

8   Create a SIGNATURE style with the following settings:

- On the ALIGNMENT tab, set the alignment to CENTER.

- On the INDENTS AND SPACING tab, set SPACING > ABOVE PARAGRAPH to 18 points (1 line),

- On the INDENTS AND SPACING tab, set SPACING > BELOW PARAGRAPH to 95 points (5 lines). Leave more space below if you have a large signature.

Creating character styles

The only character styles likely to be needed with this template are those for EMPHASIS (italics) and STRONG EMPHASIS (Bold). Base both on the Body Text (Baskervald ADF Std, 15 point). All you need to change is the STYLE on the FONT tab for the character style.

Other points

Following these steps results in a useful, well-designed template. Formatting consists of six changes of paragraph styles, two of which are automatically changed when I press the ENTER key. Instead of worrying about formatting, I can concentrate on what I am saying.

However, you may prefer to organize the paragraph styles differently than I have done, and make other adjustments beyond the basics given here.

Building a template is a matter of trial and error, and you are unlikely to remember everything – or get all design elements perfect – after a single session.

For instance, after using the template for a few letters, I realized that the default margins created a somewhat narrow look. Changing the left and right margin to 72 points (a multiple of the line spacing for the TEXT BODY) improved the layout immensely.

Similarly, when I realized the template worked best for short letters, I added a page with a footer containing the page number for longer letters.

I could also have added a few touches, such as creating and attaching a list style to the SALUTATION paragraph style that automatically added "Dear" when I applied the paragraph style.

The text style basics

The settings discussed in this chapter are the ones you are likely to use in every document. The next two chapters explore special cases and advanced settings that you may want to use now and then.

3

Text tools and traps

This chapter discusses settings that almost all documents use. This chapter is about less common character and paragraph settings. You might find several of these features mentioned here in a single document, but rarely all.

Some of these features just have limited or specialized use. However, others you should consider carefully before using.

Some are design elements that seemed reasonable decades ago when Writer was first released, but have since become obsolete – and never were (to be polite) in the best typographical tradition.

Still others are obscure or difficult to use. In these cases, the same results can often be obtained with more options by choosing another method.

There is even a feature or two that LibreOffice technically supports but implements so poorly that you will get more satisfying results if you use another piece of software instead.

I was tempted to avoid talking about such features altogether, but the warnings are worth giving. Besides, possibly, they may have more practical uses than they appear to do. If anyone knows such a use, I would be glad to hear.

Of course, if you do find a use for some of the features I disparage, ignore my cautions and do as you think best. While typographic practice can advise, it should never be a set of conventions followed blindly. In the end, anything that makes the text more readable or easier to navigate or maintain is legitimate.

Setting borders

Borders are the lines surrounding an object on all four sides. All LibreOffice's applications include an identical BORDERS tab on at least one of their styles. In Draw and Impress, a similar feature is called LINE.

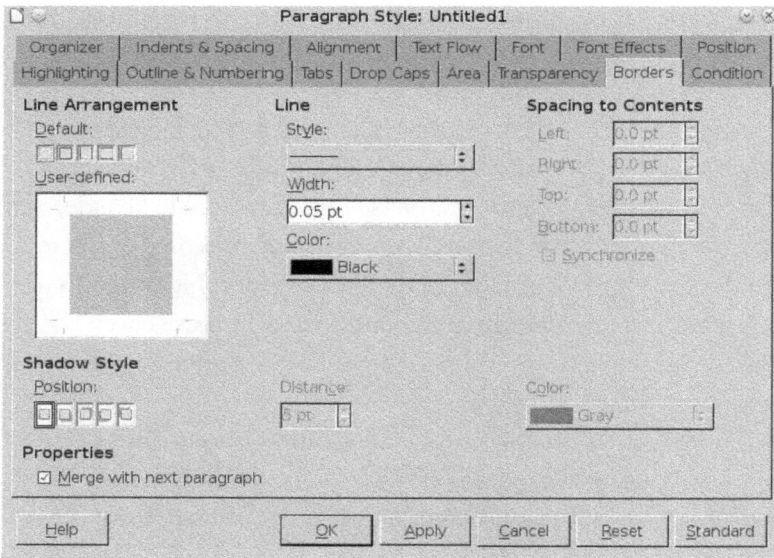

Similar BORDERS tabs are found throughout LibreOffice.

Adding borders

To set up borders:

1 Under LINE ARRANGEMENT, use either the DEFAULT or USER-DEFINED diagrams to choose on which sides you want a border.

   The DEFAULT diagram sets all sides together, offering pre-defined arrangements at a single click. With the USER-DEFINED diagram, you can set each side separately.

2 Set the line's STYLE, WIDTH, and COLOR. In most circumstances, choose the thinnest, plainest style possible. You may need to choose a thicker line so it is detectable on low-end printers.

3 Set the SPACING TO CONTENTS on each side. Generous spacing increases readability by avoiding a cramped look.

   When the SYNCHRONIZE check box is selected, you can fill in values for the LEFT and RIGHT sides or the TOP and BOTTOM sides at the same time.

Lorem ipsum dolor sit amet, consectetur adipiscing elit. Integer nec odio. Praesent libero. Sed cursus ante dapibus diam. Sed nisi. Nulla quis sem at nibh elementum imperdiet. Duis sagittis ipsum. Praesent mauris. Fusce nec tellus sed augue semper porta. Mauris massa. Vestibulum lacinia arcu eget nulla. Class aptent taciti sociosqu ad litora torquent

Lorem ipsum dolor sit amet, consectetur adipiscing elit. Integer nec odio. Praesent libero. Sed cursus ante dapibus diam. Sed nisi. Nulla quis sem at nibh elementum imperdiet. Duis sagittis ipsum. Praesent mauris. Fusce nec tellus sed augue semper porta. Mauris massa. Vestibulum lacinia arcu eget nulla. Class aptent taciti sociosqu

Above: BORDERS > SPACE TO CONTENTS set to 0 points. Below: Set to 5 points. The extra white space increases readability and prevents crowding against the borders.

Tip

Occasionally, borders may appear when you have set none. If that happens and you do not need borders, leave the LINE ARRANGEMENT blank, and select LINE > STYLE > NONE.

4 If you want a shadow as part of the border, select its POSITION, DISTANCE (from the border), and COLOR.

Caution

Shadows can help separate a picture from the background. However, if you cannot explain the reason for using a shadow, you should not use one. Shadows were so over-used in the mid-1990s that today they can look excessive and old-fashioned.

Lorem ipsum dolor sit amet, consectetur adipiscing elit. Proin bibendum maximus velit, blandit suscipit felis fermentum tristique. Aenean non neque magna. Praesent aliquam justo eros, ut aliquam arcu ullamcorper eu. In sit amet sapien non ligula pulvinar ultricies. Lorem ipsum dolor sit amet, consectetur adipiscing elit. Fusce et ullamcorper quam.

A paragraph with a border and shadow. Only use a shadow if you have a reason for doing so. The days are long past when people used shadows simply because they could.

Using borders in character and paragraph styles

Many beginning designers dislike empty space. To them, empty space is wasted space. As a result, they are tempted to corral it by putting borders around everything. This is a temptation that they should almost always avoid.

In text documents and presentation slides, the uses of borders are limited. The most obvious uses are to create a blank space to put an answer on a quiz, or to indicate a side bar in a newsletter.

Charles Darwin first explained evolution in his book ⬚.

Borders in character styles can be used for answer blanks.

Lorem ipsum dolor sit amet consectetur adipiscing elit. Integer nec odio. Praesent libero. Sed cursus ante dapibus diam. Sed nisi. Nulla quis sem at nibh elementum imperdiet. Duis sagittis ipsum. Praesent mauris. Fusce nec tellus sed augue semper porta. Mauris massa. Vestibulum lacinia arcu eget nulla. Class aptent taciti sociosqu ad litora torquent per conubia nostra, per inceptos himenaeos. Curabitur sodales ligula in libero. Sed dignissim lacinia nunc.

Curabitur tortor. Pellentesque nibh. Aenean quam. In scelerisque sem at dolor. Maecenas mattis. Sed convallis tristique sem. Proin ut ligula vel nunc egestas porttitor. Morbi lectus risus, iaculis vel, suscipit quis, luctus non, massa. Fusce ac turpis quis ligula lacinia aliquet. Mauris ipsum. Nulla metus metus, ullamcorper vel, tincidunt sed, euismod in, nibh. Quisque volutpat condimentum velit. Class aptent taciti sociosqu ad litora torquent per conubia nostra, per inceptos himenaeos. Nam nec ante.

Sed lacinia, urna non tincidunt mattis, tortor neque adipiscing diam, a cursus ipsum ante quis turpis. Nulla facilisi. Ut fringilla. Suspendisse potenti. Nunc feugiat mi a tellus consequat imperdiet. Vestibulum sapien. Proin quam. Etiam ultrices. Suspendisse in justo eu magna luctus suscipit.

Lorem ipsum dolor sit amet consectetur adipiscing elit. Integer nec odio. Praesent libero. Sed cursus ante dapibus diam. Sed nisi. Nulla quis sem at nibh elementum imperdiet. Duis sagittis ipsum.

Praesent mauris.
Fusce nec tellus sed augue semper porta. Mauris massa. Vestibulum lacinia arcu eget nulla. Class aptent taciti sociosqu ad litora torquent per conubia nostra, per inceptos himenaeos. Curabitur sodales ligula in libero. Sed dignissim lacinia nunc.

Curabitur tortor. Pellentesque nibh. Aenean quam. In scelerisque sem at dolor. Maecenas mattis. Sed convallis tristique sem. Proin ut ligula vel nunc egestas porttitor. Morbi lectus risus, iaculis vel, suscipit quis, luctus non, massa.

Fusce ac turpis quis
ligula lacinia aliquet. Mauris ipsum. Nulla metus metus, ullamcorper vel, tincidunt sed, euismod in, nibh. Quisque volutpat condimentum velit. Class aptent taciti sociosqu ad litora torquent per conubia nostra, per inceptos himenaeos. Nam nec ante.

Sed lacinia, urna non tincidunt mattis, tortor neque adipiscing diam, a cursus ipsum ante quis turpis. Nulla facilisi. Ut fringilla. Suspendisse potenti. Nunc feugiat mi a tellus consequat imperdiet.

> Lorem ipsum dolor sit amet consectetur adipiscing elit. Integer nec odio. Praesent libero. Sed cursus ante dapibus diam. Sed nisi. Nulla quis sem at nibh elementum imperdiet. Duis sagittis ipsum. Praesent mauris. Fusce nec tellus sed augue semper porta. Mauris massa. Vestibulum lacinia arcu eget nulla. Class aptent taciti sociosqu ad litora torquent per conubia nostra, per inceptos himenaeos. Curabitur sodales ligula in libero. Sed dignissim lacinia nunc.
>
> Curabitur tortor. Pellentesque nibh. Aenean quam. In scelerisque sem at dolor.

Borders in paragraph styles can be used to create side-bars. By placing a border around a small side discussion when the rest of the text has none, you emphasize that it is not part of the normal text flow. Font: Liberation Serif.

Often, however, borders are just another bit of unnecessary clutter. Enough empty space may achieve the same purpose as a border while looking less constricted. Sometimes a frame may be a better choice because it has more options.

No matter how you add borders, minimize their width and be generous with the SPACING TO CONTENTS settings. Borders that crowd the content only obscure.

Highlighting and setting backgrounds

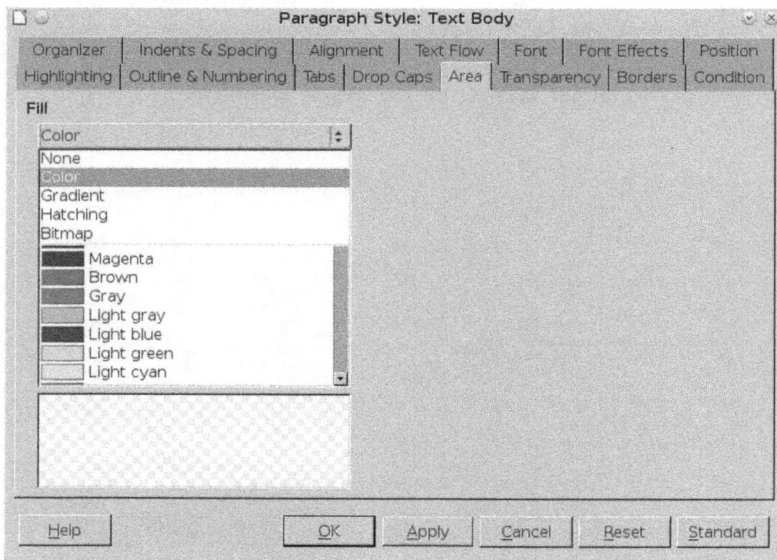

Like the BORDERS tab, the BACKGROUND/AREA tab is found throughout LibreOffice, sometimes allowing only color.

Highlighting is available in character styles, and most useful for emphasizing passages in informal documents. Backgrounds or areas are available in paragraph styles, and are basically the same feature as highlighting, except that highlighting is available only as a color, while a background or area can also be a gradient, hatching, or bitmap.

Tip

Using the AREA and TRANSPARENCY tabs, you can give a paragraph its own watermark.

If you are choosing a color background, make sure that the color you want is among LibreOffice's defined colors. If not, go to TOOLS > OPTIONS > LIBREOFFICE > COLORS to add it as a custom color, or make adjustments on the TRANSPARENCY tab (see "Setting transparency," page 44).

Similarly, before you add a graphic background, prepare its dimensions and transparency in a graphics editor such as GIMP.

The basic rule for backgrounds: text and background should contrast with each other.

For all backgrounds/areas, the basic rule is: combine light-colored text with a dark background, and dark-colored text with a light background. Without a strong contrast, your document loses readability. Dark text on a light background is easiest for many people to read, because that is the most commonly used.

Be careful, too, not to use backgrounds with too many different colors. Too often, the result will be illegibility.

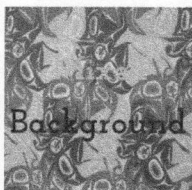

Most foreground colors are lost on multi-colored backgrounds.

Tip

When adding backgrounds, consider whether you need to check the contrast for black and white as well as color printing. The two are not necessarily the same.

Using backgrounds in character and paragraph styles

Like borders, backgrounds have limited use in character and paragraph styles. Several character styles, each with a different color background, might be useful for highlighting when you are taking notes, or for a brochure, but the majority of text-heavy documents use a plain white background.

Most of the time, you have more options and more control if you use a frame instead, or perhaps apply the background to a page style.

Setting transparency

The TRANSPARENCY tab originated in graphic styles, and was added to paragraph styles in Writer in the 4.4 release.

The tab adds transparency when a selection is made on the BACKGROUND/AREA tab. 0% is no transparency, 100% complete transparency.

From the TRANSPARENCY tab, you can:

- Create a transparency to add quickly (if approximately) another color without formally defining a color in TOOLS > OPTIONS > LIBREOFFICE > COLORS.

- Edit the transparency of a background/area to improve the contrast between the foreground and background.

- Create a background gradient using degrees of transparency. A gradient makes a transition between two colors.

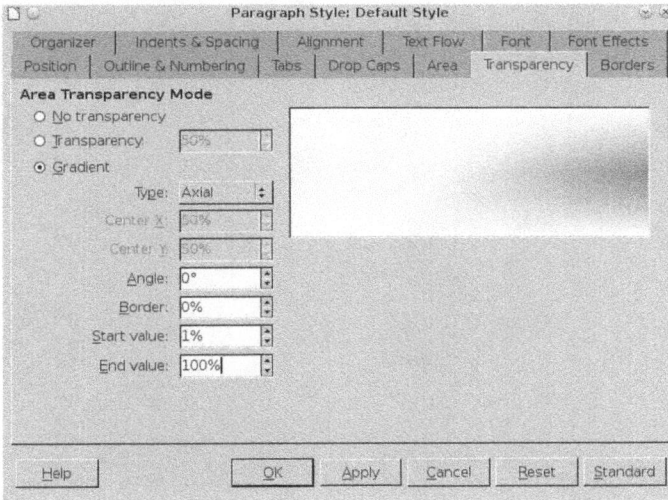

The TRANSPARENCY tab works with the AREA tab. Here, the controls to define a gradient are shown.

Setting tab stops

Tabs are set positions on a line. The place where a tab begins is called the tab position or tab stop.

Usually, tab stops should be multiples of the line-spacing, and kept to the minimum necessary. Much of the time, the standard typewriter tab stops of half or one inch will be far more than you need.

Tabs are sometimes used to create columns of text, but a table is usually a better option. If you use an automatic first line indent, in many cases the only reasons to use tab stops are from habit or because LibreOffice uses them in an advanced feature such as tables of contents.

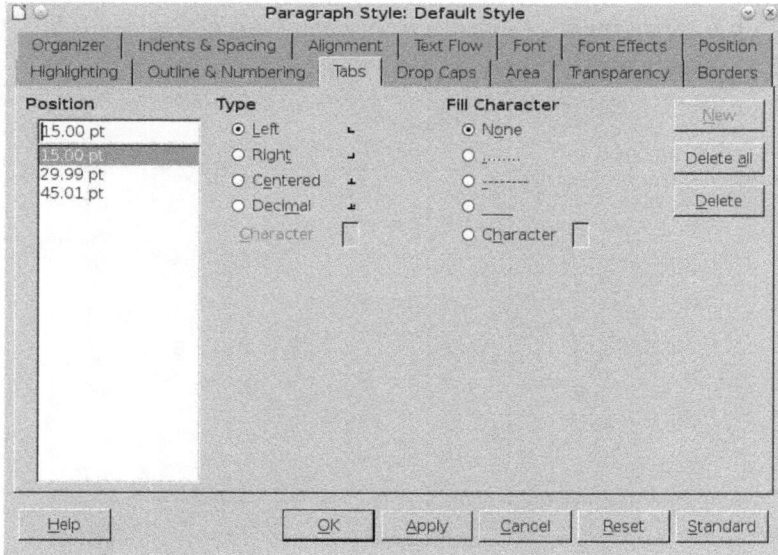

Use of tabs can be greatly minimized. When you do use tabs, make each a multiple of the line spacing.

The types of tabs are:

- LEFT: Places the left edge of the text column at the tab position, extending the text to the right. In most cases, this will be the most commonly used type, and often the only one.

- RIGHT: Places the right edge of the text at the tab, extending the text to the left. The most common use of this type is to position a column of text against the right margin.

- CENTERED: Places the center of the text at the tab position, extending it on both the left and the right. Often, this type can be replaced by setting the general alignment of the line to CENTERED.

- DECIMAL: Places the decimal at the tab position, and whole numbers and text to its left. You can set the decimal character according to the language locale. For instance, the decimal character is a period in most English locales.

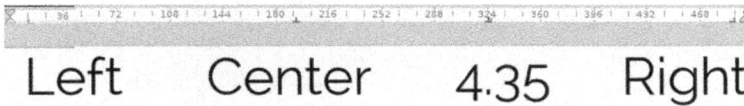

Left   Center   4.35   Right

The four types of tab positions differ in where text appears in relation to the tab stop in the ruler.

The trouble with all the types of tabs is that they can be an unstable way of positioning characters. The smallest formatting change can sometimes throw them out of position.

Using tabs effectively

Even if you minimize the use of tabs yourself, you cannot avoid LibreOffice's built-in uses of them. For example, LibreOffice uses tabs to position text in relation to bullets and numbers in list styles, and as an option in customizing tables of contents or in the use of a conditional style.

Otherwise, consider whether you need tabs or can substitute another solution. Frames or tables with invisible borders are often a more stable choice.

When using tabs, do:

- Set them in the DEFAULT paragraph styles, or at the very least, as high up the hierarchical tree as possible. Otherwise, you will have to set tabs separately for each paragraph style.

- Make the tab positions multiples of the line spacing.

- Set the tab positions as late as possible in your designing. Otherwise, changes in features such as font or font size may force you to re-set them.

When using tabs, do not:

- Use them to indicate the start of new paragraphs. Instead, create a FIRST LINE INDENT and check the AUTOMATIC box on the INDENTS AND SPACING tab.

- Use them to position characters in a text frame, such as a header or footer. Instead, use a table with invisible borders and carefully adjusted column widths.

- Use fill characters in the blank spaces between tab positions.

The Dos and Don'ts of using tab stops.

Setting up drop capitals

Drop capitals are enlarged letters that mark the start of a new chapter or section. The DROP CAPS tab for a paragraph style automates the process of creating a text frame and setting the text flow around it.

Drop caps are more common in fiction than non-fiction, and in magazines than in an academic essay. They create an informality that is more at home in a novel than in most types of non-fiction. The exception are the highly decorated capitals found in illuminated manuscripts from the Middle Ages.

Before creating drop caps, consider what other indicators of a new chapter you have in your design. If your first page style starts lower down than the rest of your pages, or if the start is marked by a recurring design or by numbers, then drop caps may be more than you need.

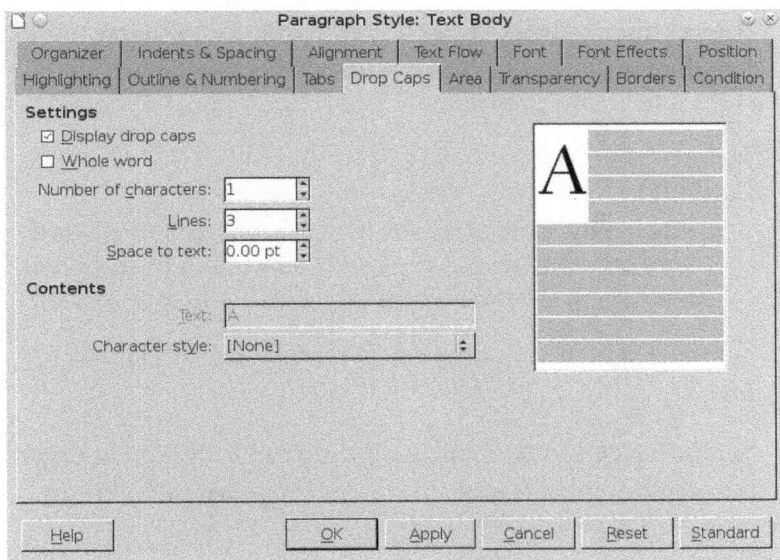

The DROP CAPS tab.

To set up drop caps:

1 Choose the font for the drop caps. It can be the same font as for body text – perhaps in a different weight – a decorative font, or even a character from a dingbat set.

2 Use the DROP CAPS character style to define the font.

3 Create a DROP CAPS paragraph style. Most likely, it will be the child of TEXT BODY, differing only in having settings for DROP CAPS.

4 On the Drop Caps tab of the paragraph style, under Settings, select Display drop caps. This selection enables others on the tab, as well as the preview to the right.

5 Under CHARACTER STYLE, select DROP CAPS.

6 Select either NUMBER OF CHARACTERS or WHOLE WORD to set the length of the drop cap. You can use up to 9 characters.

Tip

Placing the entire first line in a different font weight is a very common layout choice. If you want to try it, ignore the DROP CAPS tab and create a FIRST LINE style instead.

7 Set the height of your drop cap in terms of the number of lines.

8 Set the SPACE TO TEXT. Unless the drop cap is extremely large, the magic number is probably too much, so try half of it first.

Caution

CONTENTS > TEXT is permanently grayed-out on the DROP CAPS tab. According to the online help, the field is supposed to give the text to use instead of a single letter.

However, the WHOLE WORD and NUMBER OF CHARACTER fields substitute adequately for it.

L orem ipsum dolor sit amet, consectetur adipiscing elit. In vitae sem non erat porta vestibulum. Pellentesque ut malesuada arcu. Praesent vel lectus blandit, molestie neque a, volutpat odio. Maecenas vitae lacus hendrerit, malesuada neque nec, molestie lorem. Phasellus elit quam, interdum vel massa nec, adipiscing gravida risus. Maecenas ornare tellus vitae

Lorem ipsum dolor sit amet, consectetur adipiscing elit. In vitae sem non erat porta vestibulum. Pellentesque ut malesuada arcu. Praesent vel lectus blandit, molestie neque a, volutpat odio. Maecenas vitae lacus hendrerit, malesuada neque nec, molestie lorem. Phasellus elit quam, interdum vel massa nec, adipiscing gravida risus. Maecenas ornare tellus vitae

L orem ipsum dolor sit amet, consectetur adipiscing elit. In vitae sem non erat porta vestibulum. Pellentesque ut malesuada arcu. Praesent vel lectus blandit, molestie neque a, volutpat odio. Maecenas vitae lacus hendrerit, malesuada neque nec, molestie lorem. Phasellus elit quam, interdum vel massa nec, adipiscing gravida risus. Maecenas ornare tellus vitae

L orem ipsum dolor sit amet, consectetur adipiscing elit. In vitae sem non erat porta vestibulum. Pellentesque ut malesuada arcu. Praesent vel lectus blandit, molestie neque a, volutpat odio. Maecenas vitae lacus hendrerit, malesuada neque nec, molestie lorem. Phasellus elit quam, interdum vel massa nec, adipiscing gravida risus. Maecenas ornare tellus vitae

L orem ipsum dolor sit amet, consectetur adipiscing elit. In vitae sem non erat porta vestibulum. Pellentesque ut malesuada arcu. Praesent vel lectus blandit, molestie neque a, volutpat odio. Maecenas vitae lacus hendrerit, malesuada neque nec, molestie lorem. Phasellus elit quam, interdum vel massa nec, adipiscing gravida risus. Maecenas ornare tellus vitae

Lorem ipsum dolor sit amet, consectetur adipiscing elit. In vitae sem non erat porta vestibulum. Pellentesque ut malesuada arcu. Praesent vel lectus blandit, molestie neque a, volutpat odio. Maecenas vitae lacus hendrerit, malesuada neque nec, molestie lorem. Phasellus elit quam, interdum vel massa nec, adipiscing gravida risus. Maecenas ornare tellus vitae

L *orem ipsum dolor sit amet, consectetur adipiscing elit. In vitae sem non erat porta* vestibulum. Pellentesque ut malesuada arcu. Praesent vel lectus blandit, molestie neque a, volutpat odio. Maecenas vitae lacus hendrerit, malesuada neque nec, molestie lorem. Phasellus elit quam, interdum vel massa nec, adipiscing gravida risus. Maecenas ornare tellus vitae

A selection of drop capitals. The last sample uses a character style to place the first line in italics.

Outlining and making lists

Lists are a separate type of style in Writer. However, as you might guess from the existence of the OUTLINE & NUMBERING tab, paragraph styles are essential to lists and outlining.

Specifically, on the OUTLINE & NUMBERING tab, you can:

- Associate list styles with paragraph styles so that they can be applied automatically. The same list style can be associated with multiple paragraph styles.

- Create an outline using a single paragraph style.

- Add a paragraph style to the default outline styles so that it is listed in the Navigator, and used automatically in features like tables of contents.

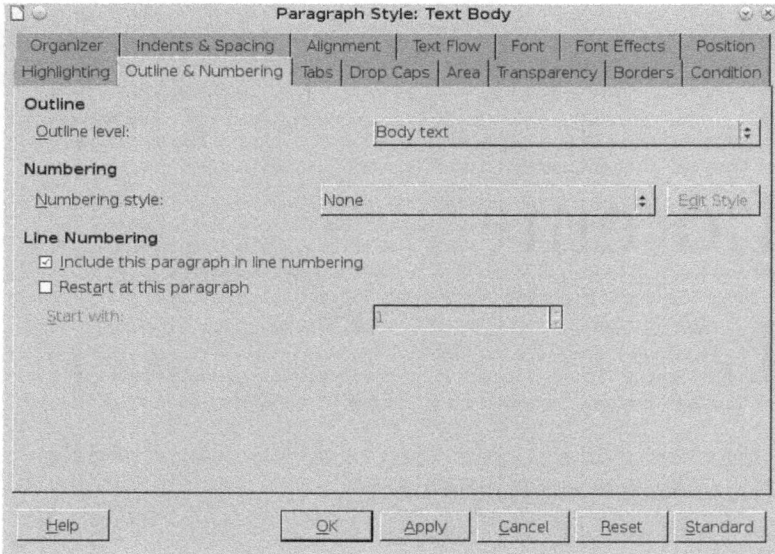

Associate a list style with a paragraph style in the NUMBERING section on a paragraph style's OUTLINE & NUMBERING tab.

Automating lists

An unordered list is another name for a bullet list, and an ordered list is another name for a numbered list.

Set up an ordered or unordered list in the dialog for list styles .
Then associate it with a paragraph style from the paragraph's
OUTLINE & NUMBERING tab in the NUMBERING STYLE field.

Restarting paragraph numbering

You do not need to create a separate list style for each
numbered list in a document.

To restart the numbering in any numbered list, select RESTART
NUMBERING from a paragraph's right-click menu.

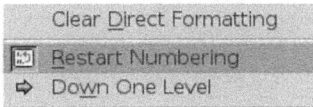

Clear <u>D</u>irect Formatting
🔢 <u>R</u>estart Numbering
⇨ Do<u>w</u>n One Level

Restart the numbering in a list from the right-click menu.

Caution

The RESTART AT THIS PARAGRAPH field on the OUTLINE &
NUMBERING tab is for line numbering, not paragraph
numbering.

Nesting lists

A nested list – a list within a list – is most common in an
online text, where space is unimportant and structured text like
lists and tables improve readability.

To nest a list, you have two choices. The first is to create a list
style, and set up two or more list levels with different formatting
choices on the POSITION and OPTIONS tabs. The advantage of list
levels is that each level can be formatted separately, but all the
levels remain connected. You can switch to the next level below
by pressing the TAB key, or to the one above by pressing
SHIFT+TAB.

The preview pane can help you set up each list level, and the customized list style is associated with a paragraph style for use.

To switch to a lower list level while using the associated paragraph style, press the TAB key before entering content; to switch to a higher list level, press SHIFT+TAB.

The PREVIEW pane for a bulleted list style with two list levels. The other list levels have not been customized, so they default to the same bullet as the top level.

The second choice is to create two separate list styles, then associate each list style with a separate paragraph style.

Neither choice has any advantage over the other, since you are still dealing with the same options. However, in both cases, each nested list is typically indented more than the list level above it. Typically, too, each list level will use a different bullet style or numbering system.

Style names like BULLETED and BULLETED 2 or NESTED will help to remind you of the relation between the two paragraph styles. For convenience, use the same names for both the PARAGRAPH and LIST styles, since they cannot be mixed up.

1ˢᵗ list style   1. Lorem ipsum dolor sit amet, consectetur adipiscing elit.

                2. Sed et urna ac lorem malesuada venenatis ut et lorem.

2ⁿᵈ list style   • Phasellus imperdiet lorem turpis, at egestas neque egestas nec.

                • Vestibulum a nibh ante.

                • Sed accumsan orci at turpis tempor, sit amet pulvinar ipsum vehicula.

1ˢᵗ list style   3. Tincidunt ac magna.

Nested lists created using two separate list styles.

Outlining with paragraph styles

LibreOffice has several ways to outline using paragraph styles. With TOOLS > OUTLINE NUMBERING, you can choose a numbering style for each paragraph style, making it part of the Outline Levels (see "Outlining and making lists," page 51). Alternatively, you can ignore TOOLS > OUTLINE NUMBERING, and associate each Heading style with a separate list style using the STYLES AND FORMATTING window.

An even easier form of outlining is to create a single list style for outlining. If you want to, you can manually set up the different levels on the list style's OPTIONS tab. However, you can get much the same result by selecting a pre-defined pattern from the list style's OUTLINE tab instead.

To use the paragraph style, press ENTER + TAB to add a sub-level paragraph. The sub-level paragraph automatically uses the numbering pattern of the list style. To raise the level of a paragraph style, press ENTER + TAB + SHIFT.

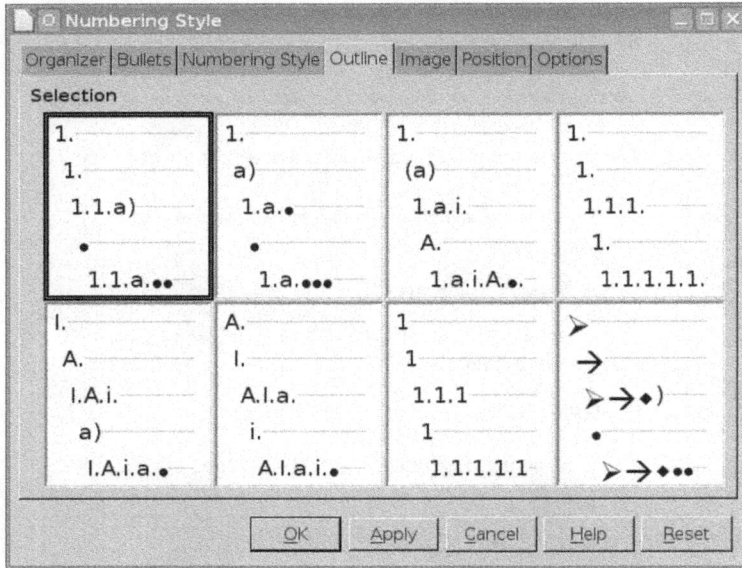

Numbering Style			_ □ ✕

Organizer | Bullets | Numbering Style | Outline | Image | Position | Options

Selection

1.
  1.
    1.1.a)
     •
      1.1.a.••
	1.
	  a)
	    1.a.•
	     •
	      1.a.•••
		1.
		  (a)
		    1.a.i.
		     A.
		      1.a.i.A.•.
			1.
			  1.
			    1.1.1.
			     1.
			      1.1.1.1.1.

I.
  A.
    I.A.i.
     a)
      I.A.i.a.•
	A.
	  I.
	    A.I.a.
	     i.
	      A.I.a.i.•
		1
		  1
		    1.1.1
		     1
		      1.1.1.1.1
			➤
			  →
			    ➤→•)
			     •
			      ➤→••

OK | Apply | Cancel | Help | Reset

The pre-defined formatting for outlines in the list styles window. An outline is typically a way of planning a document that readers never see, so often whether the pre-defined format is exactly what you prefer won't matter.

Creating outlines with a single paragraph style

To set up a single paragraph style for outlining:

1 Create a list style and associate it with one of the pre-defined formats on the OUTLINE tab.

2 Select or make a paragraph style for outlining. You cannot use the HEADING 1-10 styles. Presumably, this restriction prevents confusion between a single paragraph style outline and the registered outline levels.

3 On the ORGANIZER tab of the paragraph style, set the style to use itself as the NEXT STYLE.

4 Assign the list style to the paragraph style using the NUMBERING field on the paragraph style's OUTLINE & NUMBERING tab.

Adding paragraph styles to outline levels

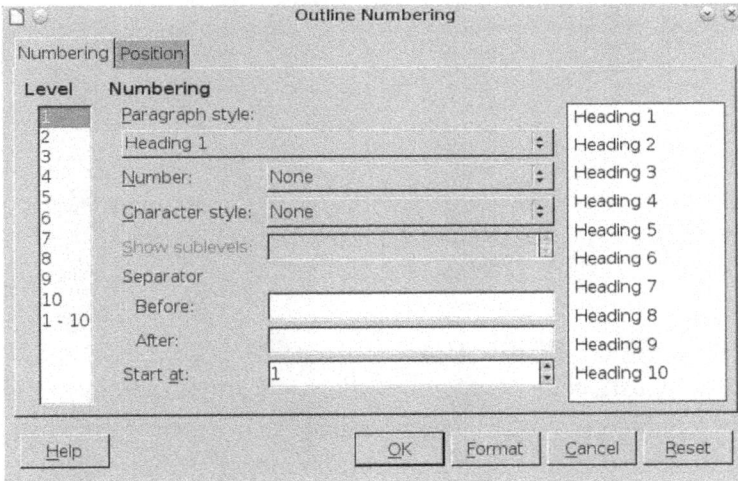

OUTLINE LEVELS default to Heading paragraph styles. You can add other paragraph styles using the OUTLINE LEVEL field on their OUTLINE & NUMBERING tabs.

Tip

In the drop-down list for the OUTLINE LEVEL field on the OUTLINE & NUMBERING tab, all paragraph styles not assigned to an outline level are identified as BODY TEXT. This designation has nothing to do with the TEXT BODY paragraph style.

Outline levels are a concept used throughout LibreOffice to automate advanced features. For example, outline levels determine which paragraph styles are displayed by default in the Navigator under HEADINGS, and in a table of contents .

By default, outline levels are mapped to the HEADING 1-10 paragraph styles. OUTLINE LEVEL 1 is mapped to HEADING 1, and so on.

You can change these mappings, or add another paragraph style to an outline level in the OUTLINE LEVEL field on the OUTLINE & NUMBERING tab.

Tip

You can assign more than one paragraph style to an outline level, but only one paragraph style displays in TOOLS > OUTLINE NUMBERING.

Skipping a paragraph in a list

In many lists, each paragraph is a list item and is therefore numbered. However, you sometimes need to break up a list with an unnumbered or unbulleted paragraph that gives more detail about a list item. Without such a paragraph, a list item may turn into a long paragraph, reducing the readability that is the whole point of using a list.

To create a style for such paragraphs, you can use the paragraph style with a list to create a linked paragraph that is mostly formatted identically. The exceptions are on the OUTLINE & NUMBERING tab, on which:

- OUTLINE LEVEL is set to BODY TEXT.

- NUMBERING STYLE is set to NONE.

- THIS PARAGRAPH IN LINE NUMBERING is unchecked.

If you have only a few horizontal indents, this style may be usable with multiple lists.

BODY TEXT INDENT is a pre-defined paragraph style that you can use for this purpose.

Tip

If you want to number paragraphs as lines in a poem, use TOOLS > LINE NUMBERING.

This tool is more comprehensive than the formatting available from within paragraph style formatting, with a selection of character styles and the exact positioning of numbers in relation to text.

Using multiple languages

LibreOffice supports over 110 languages, and many more locales. Locales are variants of a language that have unique vocabularies and spellings.

For example, in the United Kingdom English locale, the correct spelling is "neighbours," while in United States English, it is "neighbors." A complete locale consists of separate dictionaries for spell-checking, hyphenation, and thesauruses.

Many users use only the default language determined by the version of LibreOffice that they downloaded. However, you have two options for adding support for more languages and locales.

The most common way to add support for additional languages is to select them from the drop-down list at TOOLS > OPTIONS > LANGUAGE SETTINGS > WRITING AIDS > USER-DEFINED DICTIONARIES > NEW.

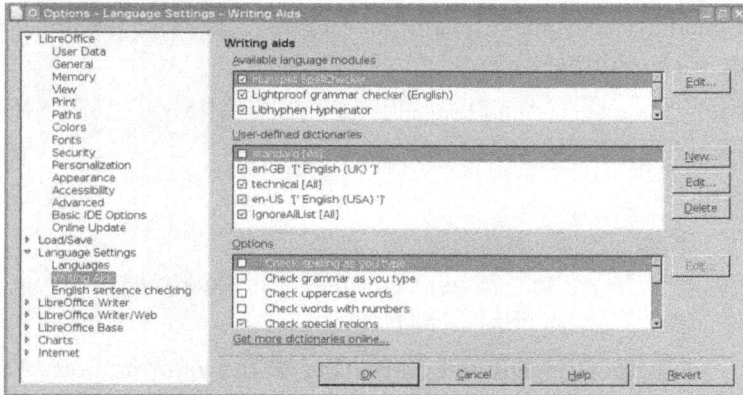

Use the general language settings to load as many languages and locales as you want.

In addition, the extension site also has packages for several languages, including Ancient Greek, Finnish, and Basque.

You can update extensions with TOOLS > EXTENSION MANAGER > NEW, which is an advantage when the dictionaries are still being developed and changing rapidly.

Setting up other language features

Adding dictionary locales may be only the first step in using another language. You may need to:

- Select a system keyboard layout for the language. An international English keyboard is adequate for most Western European languages. Without a suitable keyboard layout, you have to rely on INSERT > SPECIAL CHARACTER for accents and umlauts.

- Install a font for a language. A Greek style is of limited use if your installation of LibreOffice has no Greek font installed.

- Adjust the settings for East Asian or Bi-Directional Languages at TOOLS > OPTIONS > LANGUAGE SETTINGS > LANGUAGES > ENHANCED LANGUAGE SUPPORT.

- Create multiple styles with similar names in a multi-language document. For example, you might have paragraph styles called TEXT BODY – ENGLISH and TEXT BODY – FRENCH.

- Disable TOOLS > AUTOCORRECT OPTIONS in a multi-language document. If you don't use Autocorrect, uncheck the ENABLE WORD COMPLETION and COLLECT WORDS boxes at TOOLS > AUTOCORRECT OPTIONS > WORD COMPLETION.

- Set URLs or snippets of code to NONE in the LANGUAGE FIELD to spare yourself extra queries while spell checking.

Creating a block quote style

All forms of academic quotation have a special format for long quotations – that is, quotations that fill more than three lines or are longer than about 100 words.

Quotations that meet this criteria are presented in a block so that they are easier to read. The assumption is that a long quote would not be used unless it was important. Readers may wonder if the emphasis is misplaced if a block quotation is not especially relevant.

Typically, the paragraph style for a block quote is the child of the body text style. The standard format for a block quotation is:

- Do not use quotation marks, unless someone is quoted directly or speaking.

- Use the same font and font size as for the body text. Making the font size smaller only makes the block harder to read.

- Use an equal indentation on the left and right sides of the paragraph, based on the line spacing. Usually, 40–50 points on each side will be about right, the exact width depending on the font size.

> Lorem ipsum dolor sit amet, consectetur adipiscing elit. Praesent consequat tincidunt eros, nec dictum nulla ultrices in. Suspendisse id pharetra massa. Donec egestas massa nulla, eleifend hendrerit odio consectetur facilisis:
>
> Fusce eget mattis augue. Sed sit amet semper lacus, eu malesuada lectus. Cras sodales faucibus ipsum. quis lobortis tellus.
>
> In ac commodo mi. Ut ac semper lectus. Vestibulum ante ipsum primis in faucibus orci luctus et ultrices posuere cubilia Curae; Vestibulum ante ipsum primis in faucibus orci luctus et ultrices posuere cubilia Curae.
>
> Sed nec neque vitae dolor auctor hendrerit. Aenean tempus in risus vitae gravida. Ut pretium porttitor nulla. auctor commodo quam ultrices eu.

The standard layout for a block quotation. The extra indentation is used instead of quotation marks.

- Indicate new paragraphs by either a first line indent or else an extra space between paragraphs. The indicator is not necessarily the same as the one used in the rest of the body text.

Writer includes a QUOTATIONS paragraph style by default, although you might prefer a custom style with a name like BLOCK QUOTATION for greater clarity.

Preparing styles for HTML

HTML has never been well integrated into LibreOffice Writer.

On the one hand, Writer includes VIEW > WEB LAYOUT so you can have an approximation of how an HTML page looks, but the view is not always reliable. It also includes VIEW > HTML SOURCE so you can see the code with which you are working.

Character and Paragraph Styles

On the other hand, you cannot save files as HTML in the template manager.

To add to the confusion, HTML is treated in a very individualist way. While LibreOffice uses FILE > DOCUMENT PROPERTIES to create a thorough collection of meta-tags, it also converts all graphics to .jpegs, with no provision for doing otherwise.

An even greater limitation is that only a limited number of character and paragraph styles are converted directly into HTML tags. Other styles, as well as fields, are converted to .css classes.

These peculiarities mean that HTML files exported from LibreOffice preserve as much of the formatting as possible.

Unfortunately, they also mean that LibreOffice does not produce clean HTML – that is, files with only HTML tags that are easy to use in other applications.

```
<!DOCTYPE HTML PUBLIC "-//W3C//DTD HTML 4.0 Transitional//EN">
<html>
<head>
  <meta http-equiv="content-type" content="text/html; charset=utf-8"/>
  <title>designing-with-libreoffice</title>
  <meta name="generator" content="LibreOffice 4.4.0.3 (Linux)"/>
  <meta name="author" content="Bruce Byfield"/>
  <meta name="created" content="2015-03-10T16:43:53.833362432"/>
  <meta name="changedby" content="Bruce Byfield"/>
  <meta name="changed" content="2015-03-12T14:27:31.680201186"/>
  <style type="text/css">
    @page:left { size: 432pt 648pt; margin-left: 88pt; margin-right: 64pt; margin-top:
72pt; margin-bottom: 88pt }
    @page:right { size: 432pt 648pt; margin-left: 88pt; margin-right: 64pt; margin-top:
72pt; margin-bottom: 88pt }
    @page:first { }
    p { text-indent: 24pt; margin-bottom: 0pt; line-height: 16pt; orphans: 2; widows: 2;
page-break-before: auto }
```

Looking at the source code for HTML generated by LibreOffice shows how cluttered it can be.

Unless you are prepared to write your own style sheet, or clean up HTML files exported from LibreOffice either manually or through a program like HTML Tidy, LibreOffice's exported

HTML requires great effort while offering results that are usually mediocre at best.

You could, of course, create a series of macros for HTML tags, then save files as plain text, renaming them in a file manager. However, at that point, using a dedicated HTML editor is less trouble.

The only times that using LibreOffice's HTML output is advisable are when the output is only going to be used by itself and has a short life.

Problems with cluttered HTML are often compounded when the output files are used, or when someone uses a file without knowing its limitations.

Paragraph style	HTML tags	Comments
Heading 1–6	<h1> – <h6>	Notice that only 6 headings are available, while Writer has 10.
List Contents	<p>	Converts to the default paragraph tag. Use with list styles.
List Headings	<dl>, <dd>	Creates a definition list <dl> or adds the heading <dd>.
Preformatted text	<pre>	Appears in the web browser in a monospaced font (such as Courier).
Quotations	<blockquote>	Indents the text on both margins.
Sender	<address>	

Table Contents	<p>	Converts to the default paragraph tag.
Table Heading	<p>	Converts to the default paragraph tag.
Text body	<p>	The default HTML tag for contents.

How Paragraph styles are mapped to HTML tags.

Character style	HTML tags	Comments
Definition	<dfn>	Displays default font.
Emphasis	<em>	Displays as an italic font.
Endnote characters	References style sheet.	Defaults to default font.
Example	<samp>	Defaults to monospaced font.
Footnote characters	References style sheet.	Uses default font.

How Character styles are mapped to HTML tags.

Minimizing HTML problems

LibreOffice HTML code is generally best avoided. However, if you do decide to use it, follow these steps to minimize problems:

1   Select FILE > NEW > HTML DOCUMENT.

2   Press F11 to open the STYLES AND FORMATTING window. Notice that the ALL and HTML views are identical.

3   Select VIEW > WEB LAYOUT. This selection displays the file as a web page instead of a printed page.

4   Customize only by making changes to the pre-defined paragraph and character styles listed in the table above.

Tip

If you want clean code, avoid using additional styles, using any character or paragraph style that requires a style sheet, or using multiple page, frame, or list styles.

In other words, design as though you are using the plainest possible HTML.

5   Save the document by selecting FILE > SAVE AS and selecting HTML DOCUMENT TEMPLATE (.OTT) as the format or file type. Notice that you cannot save an HTML document using TEMPLATES > SAVE AS TEMPLATE. If you try, you receive no error message, but nothing is saved. Instead, save the file as an HTML DOCUMENT TEMPLATE in a directory specifically set aside for that purpose.

6   If you want clean HTML output, do one (or both) of the following: Manually remove unnecessary tags or run the file through a tool such as HTML Tidy. In Linux, many major distributions have HTML Tidy in their repositories.

7   Open the file in at least one major browser such as Chrome, Firefox, or Microsoft Edge to see whether any display problems exist.

To use the template, navigate to the directory in which the template was saved.

Tip

If these instructions seem too complicated, avoid using Writer to generate HTML output. On all operating platforms, there are many tools for writing web pages that are easier to use than Writer.

Moving beyond practical text

If you are reading this book from beginning to end, at this point all the features of character and paragraph styles that you might want to use regularly have been covered.

The next chapter discusses some advanced features – ones that are not strictly necessary to your design, but ones that can automate your design and make template design more efficient.

4

Positioning and automating text

This chapter concludes the discussion about character and paragraph styles by talking about their advanced features. It explains the relationship between paragraph and list styles, how to position characters more precisely, and several specific ways to automate your work flows using text styles.

The automating features are easy to overlook, but they can be as important as features that affect the look of a document.

For example, a conditional style allows you to format the same style differently depending on its context, or set a paragraph style so that it always starts a new page. Although casual users may never be aware of such features, those who write as part of their work will soon become well aware of the time these feature save.

You will rarely use these features all the time, nor all of them at once. However, knowing what is available can help you to design your documents more intelligently and to work more efficiently when you write.

For example, the font effect HIDE sounds minor. Yet in one unimportant-looking toggle switch, HIDE provides an elegant solution for one of the most difficult tasks for professional documenters – maintaining multiple versions of the same document in a single file.

Fine-tuning characters

Like most word processors or layout software, LibreOffice does much of the housekeeping for design.

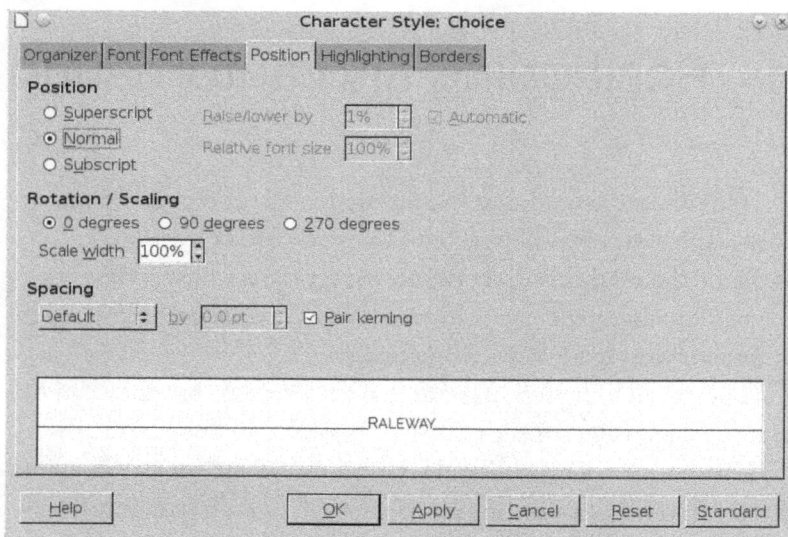

Unique to character styles, the POSITION tab is the main spot for adjusting individual characters.

For example, without consulting users, Writer examines font files to display characters properly. It also detects whether a font family includes italics or bold weights, and decides the size and placement of footnote numbers.

Most users are happy to let LibreOffice make these decisions. However, the software's decisions are not always ideal, so at times you might want to tweak the spacing between characters or reposition footnote numbers.

LibreOffice includes the tools you need for such tweaking. Many are on the POSITION tab for character styles, although others are scattered throughout the character and paragraph style dialogs.

Positioning superscript and subscript

The POSITION tab of a character style gives you several advanced options for adjusting superscript characters (above others on the same line) and subscript characters (below others on the same line). Another alternative for superscript characters is to adjust the vertical alignment of text on the same line (see "Aligning different-sized text on one line," page 73).

These adjustments are relatively common, because, depending on the font, LibreOffice's default superscript and subscript characters can sometimes be too too small for easy reading.

To understand superscript and subscript characters, you have to remember that all letters sit on an imaginary baseline. Many characters have what is called an x-height – the height of a letter x, but also of an m or r, as well as the bowl of a lower case b or p.

Still others like y have descenders, or lines that are lower than the baseline, while letters like k have ascenders, or lines that rise above the x-height. However, all characters are positioned relative to the baseline. The exact positions are part of the font's design and are stored in its files. There is no reason, though, why you should not modify the intended design if you care to make the effort.

---

letter height — superscript — ascender

$$y^2 = ?\quad h_2o$$

x-height · baseline · descender · subscript

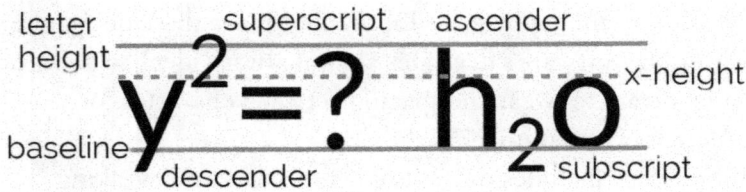

Superscript and subscript characters. The superscript "2" on the left is higher than the ascenders or the question mark, and throws off the look of the line.

By contrast, the subscript "2" on the right is as low as the bottom of the descender on the "y," which gives a more consistent look to the line (Font: Lato).

Superscript characters, such as mathematical components or footnote numbers, are usually positioned somewhere between the x-height and the height of the ascenders.

Similarly, subscript characters, such as those in chemical equations, usually sit between the baseline and the low point of descenders.

The size of superscript and subscript characters is a trade off between being large and easily readable and being uncluttered but harder to read. To many users, LibreOffice's defaults are too small.

When adjusting both position and size, be prepared for several trials and errors before getting the best results, with the adjustments getting smaller as you move closer to the ideal.

To direct your experiments, consider these points:

- The exact size will vary with the font's white space, but 40–60% of the body text should be the usual range.

- If a font's characters use a lot of white space, so that they look small compared to fonts of the same size, increase its size.

Character and Paragraph Styles

- Unless the x-height is exceptionally large, using it for the bottom of superscript characters often makes for a consistent design. However, using this guide with a large x-height is likely to make the superscript characters too small.

- Avoid old style characters for superscript and subscript. Their lack of a common baseline means either an eye-disturbing clutter or a time-consuming positioning of each numeral separately.

- Aligning superscript characters with the top of ascenders and subscript characters with the bottom of descenders has the advantage of being symmetrical while giving you a visible target.

STOP
Caution
The fields for lowering or raising superscript or subscript characters read all input as percentages, rounded to the nearest number. You cannot use points in them.

STOP
Caution
The POSITION tab for characters and paragraph styles is specifically for blocks of text. To create formulas, open FILE > NEW > FORMULA or use the Math application.

Aligning different-sized text on one line

The TEXT-TO-TEXT option on the ALIGNMENT tab vertically aligns text of different sizes on the same line. It can be used with a brochure or poster than an essay, but its main use is probably to create superscript or subscript characters without the fuss of using the POSITION tab (see "Positioning superscript and subscript," page 71).

The setting can align font sizes by the TOP, MIDDLE, or BOTTOM of the letters, or the default BASE LINE. In each case, the largest characters remain on the baseline, while other characters are raised or lowered in relation to them. For example, if you select BOTTOM, then the smaller characters are positioned at the bottom of the largest characters' descenders (the lines below the base line). Similarly, with TOP selected, the smaller characters are positioned at the top of the largest characters' ascenders (the lines above the x-height).

However, mostly you can leave the setting on AUTOMATIC, which defaults so that all different font sizes are aligned by the base line. In other words, you can usually safely ignore the setting.

lorem ipsum lorem ipsum lorem ipsum

lorem ipsum lorem ipsum lorem ipsum

lorem ipsum lorem ipsum lorem ipsum

lorem ipsum lorem ipsum lorem ipsum

From top to bottom: The TEXT-TO-TEXT field on the ALIGNMENT tab set to AUTOMATIC (BASE LINE), BOTTOM, MIDDLE, AND TOP.

Rotating text

The POSITION tab for character style includes settings for rotating text 90 (right angle to the baseline and above) and 270 degrees (right angle to the baseline and below). These settings are mostly useful in a table heading, but both interfere with readability and should not be used if any alternative exists.

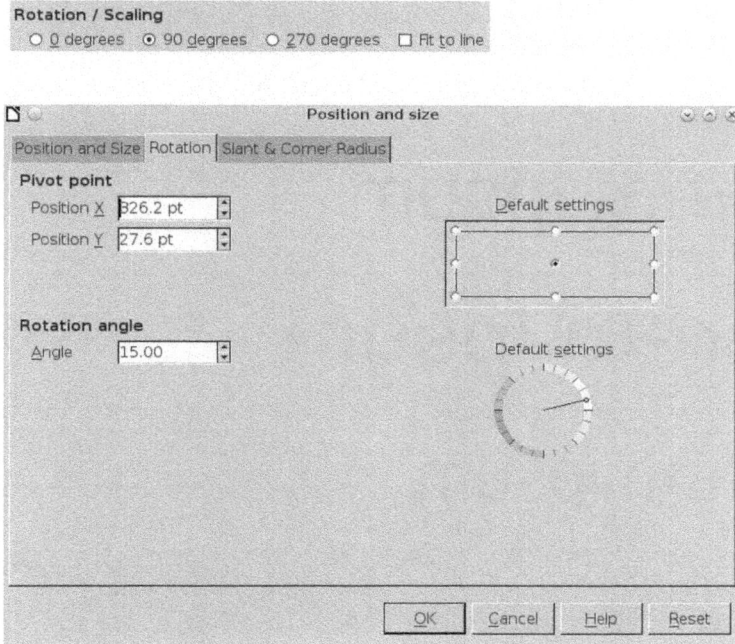

Rotation / Scaling
○ 0 degrees ⊙ 90 degrees ○ 270 degrees ☐ Fit to line

Above: Controls for rotating a character style on the POSITION tab. Below: Controls for rotating graphic text on a sample's right-click menu. Graphic text is text created with the DRAWING toolbar, and is treated as a drawing object rather than as text.

The rotation tools may be useful in brochure and ad designs, but they are very basic. You will have more precision than these settings offer if you use graphical text – text treated as a drawing object – and then right-click and select POSITION AND SIZE > ROTATION instead.

Adjusting font width

The width of characters is interpreted by LibreOffice's reading of each font's file. However, you can adjust it using the SCALE WIDTH field on the POSITION tab. This feature is especially useful when you have no condensed or expanded version in a font family.

lorem ipsum

lorem ipsum

lorem ipsum

From top to bottom: 100%, 115%, and 85% character width. Greater increases or decreases tend to look clumsy with most fonts, especially at smaller sizes. Font: Maven Pro.

In pre-digital typesetting, changing the width of a font would also include changing the design of many of the individual characters to keep the proportions in the shape of the letter. These adjustments do not happen with most digital fonts, and rarely to the same degree. Consequently, you can do little to change the width of some fonts without producing a disordered mess.

However, most fonts can stand 1–15% adjustments less or more than the default 100% without deteriorating too badly. These adjustments can help improve the page color of the body text.

Adjusting character combinations (kerning)

Kerning is the spacing between characters. Professional printers sometimes adjust kerning to improve the appearance of awkward combinations of letters. Combinations such as "Va," "ll," and "ff" can be improved in most fonts, and individual fonts may benefit from the adjustment of other combinations as well.

VaVa ffff llll

Changing the spacing between characters using the SPACING field on the POSITION tab.

Left: Reducing the space between characters improves the spacing.

Middle: Creating your own ligature by moving characters together.

Right: Sometimes, kerning means increasing the space between characters for easier reading. Font: Maven Pro.

Kerning has always been a concern in typography, but digital typography makes it more important than ever. Unlike in manual type, digital fonts usually do not have different spacing when the font size changes. Instead, the spacing is intended for a standard size.

Consequently, if you greatly decrease or increase font size, the kerning may be off. What is intended for 12 points may not work for 8 or 48 points.

Moreover, LibreOffice's general kerning tends to be very loose, and you can often improve on it if you are willing to make the effort and make small changes.

If you choose to handle your own kerning, create character styles with adjusted spacing. You may manage with only a single

---

kerning character style for all your needs, but if you are really attentive to detail, you might decide on individual kerning character styles for different letter combinations – it all depends on your patience, the font you use, and your perfectionism.

However, you may want to change the spacing, either to improve legibility or for a short string of characters in a more graphical document, such as a brochure, by adjusting the SPACING field on the POSITION tab.

If you are manually adjusting justified lines, you might also want to make micro changes here and there.

No matter what your interest, you will want to select the PAIR kerning box beside the field.

Tip

Whether you worry about kerning depends on how much of a perfectionist not only you, but the font's designer, happens to be.

Often, you can reduce the amount of kerning by carefully choosing a font after looking at letter combinations that often need kerning. Gentium, for instance, is tightly kerned and even uses ligatures automatically.

By contrast, early versions of Cantarell had a reputation – since outgrown – for being poorly kerned, which made manual kerning much more difficult.

Manufacturing small capitals

Small capitals are designed to improve the look of two or more capital letters in a row. Although they have to be applied in individual cases, small caps are especially useful in improving the readability of text full of abbreviations.

SMALL CAPS

MANUFACTURED
REGULAR CAPS

From top to bottom: genuine small caps, manufactured small caps, and regular caps. If you compare the "A" in the genuine small caps with the other samples, you can see that small caps are not just a matter of size – the proportions of letters are also changed. Font: Linux Libertine G.

Although LibreOffice 5.3 and later can apply small caps accurately for fonts that use the OpenType format, if you are using a font in the older TrueType format, LibreOffice creates an imitation of them, usually making them smaller than ordinary capitals. However, these imitations are rarely more than adequate, because true small capitals are distinguished not just by size, but by major redesigns of characters. In fact, they can be so bad that you may prefer to avoid using them at all.

If you want small capitals with a TrueType font, you are probably better off making your own. The results will be less than perfect, but probably better than the ones LibreOffice manufactures.

Making your own small caps

If a font lacks small capitals, LibreOffice manufactures some. However, you might want to see if you can improve on what

LibreOffice offers. If so, follow these steps to manufacture small caps for yourself:

1   Use the regular capitals for your experiments. Starting from manufactured capitals likely means that you are inheriting all sorts of problems that are hard to pin down.

2   Start with a character style that is several points smaller than the paragraph font with which it will be used. Experiment until you find a suitable size.

3   Use the SCALE WIDTH field on the POSITION tab to make the characters slightly wider than those of the paragraph style it will accompany. Do not increase the width by more than a few percent, or it may look grotesque.

4   Increasing the width may have upset the spacing between characters, so experiment with the SPACING field on the POSITION tab. Because the small cap character style has a smaller font size, you probably will want to increase the spacing anyway to increase legibility.

When you have finished your tweaks, compare your effort to LibreOffice's manufactured small caps, and choose the best one to use.

Making line spacing consistent

Even advanced users puzzle over the REGISTER-TRUE setting on the INDENTS & SPACING tab. It's a large mystery for a simple setting. The REGISTER-TRUE feature makes lines consistent across the pages – or as near as possible if different-sized fonts are used.

When REGISTER-TRUE is selected, the lines of text in columns, mirrored pages, or on both sides of a page are spaced identically.

The setting improves the looks of both single and multi-column documents, and prevents shadows of the other side being from interfering with reading.

Usually, the spacing is that of the TEXT BODY font.

Tip

Setting REGISTER-TRUE for more than one paragraph style can negates the setting. Use the setting only for the paragraph style used most often – usually, TEXT BODY – and related styles – for example, TEXT BODY INDENT – that use the same line spacing.

Instead of using REGISTER-TRUE for Headings, make the font size, the space above, and the space below equal a multiple of the line spacing. That way, the Headings will rarely be out of sync for any length of time.

You can improve the effectiveness of the setting for pages printed on both sides by choosing a heavier weight of paper – which you probably want anyway if a document is important enough that you are concerned about line spacing.

There is no reason not to select this setting, but setting LINE SPACING to FIXED on the INDENTS & SPACING tab will produce much the same effect.

Tip

Page styles also have a REGISTER-TRUE setting, which allows you to set the line spacing by page, selecting the paragraph style to use. Choose the paragraph or the page REGISTER-TRUE setting, rather than using both.

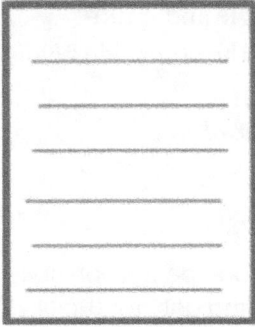

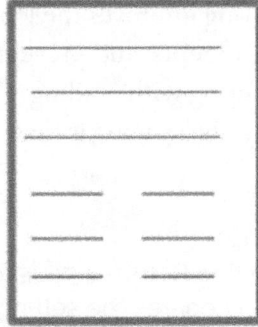

The REGISTER-TRUE feature on the INDENTS & SPACING tab makes lines consistent across the pages – or as near as possible if different-sized fonts are used.

Automating with styles

People think of typography mostly in terms of format – that is, the choices of fonts and spacing. However, digital typography is also about making a document easier to construct and maintain.

These concerns do not matter if you are writing a document that will be sent, read, and discarded in a matter of minutes. In fact, any attempt to implement them in a short-lived document is a waste of effort.

However, many other documents have longer life spans. For example, a technical manual may be revised a dozen times or more in its life cycle. In such circumstances, any formatting that gives you one less thing to think about is welcome.

This section introduces two features of paragraph styles that make documents easier to construct: using conditional styles, and setting page breaks by style.

In exchange for some extra setup, both features keep your hands on the keyboard as you work, allowing you to focus on content instead of distracting you with formatting issues.

Character and Paragraph Styles

Configuring conditional styles

A conditional style is an alternative way of using paragraph styles. Normally, you define a style, then set the NEXT STYLE field on the ORGANIZER tab.

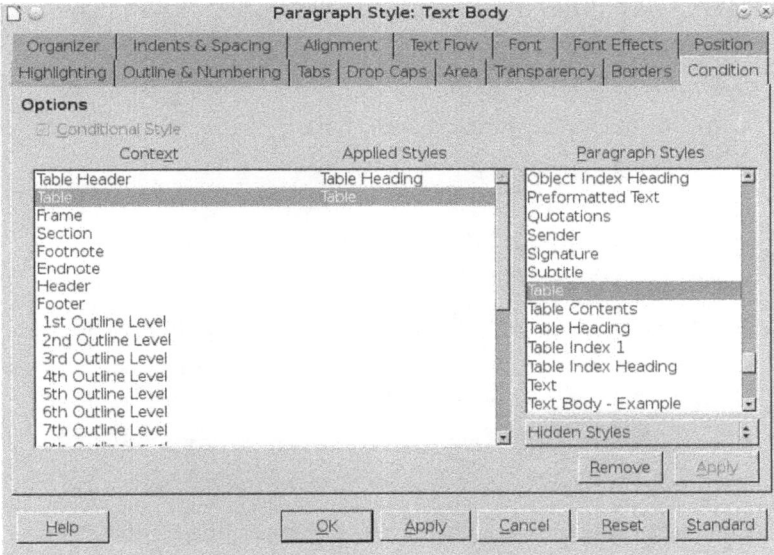

The CONDITION tab sets up one paragraph style to use the formatting of other styles in different contexts.

However, with a conditional style, you define the paragraph's format in each context, such as in a table or a footer. When the cursor moves to a new context, the style's format changes automatically.

STOP Caution

Don't confuse a conditional paragraph style with a CONDITIONAL TEXT field available from INSERT > FIELDS. All that the two have in common is that each changes when their context changes.

Conditional styles are different enough from the normal use of styles that they puzzle many users, who scrupulously avoid them. However, they are easier to use than you might imagine. Each contextual format is defined by another paragraph style, then connected to the conditional style on the CONDITION tab.

Conditional styles do have limitations:

- You cannot make any pre-defined paragraph styles conditional except TEXT BODY. In fact, pre-defined paragraph styles display no CONDITION tab, although new (custom) paragraph styles created from them do.

- If you want a custom style to be conditional, you must set up at least one condition before you click the OK or ACCEPT button when you close the style dialog window for the first time. Otherwise, the next time you open the style's dialog window, the CONDITION tab is no longer available.

- A conditional style is limited to thirty pre-defined contexts. You might be able to think of at least two dozen more contexts that might be useful, but you cannot create custom contexts.

Still, even with these limitations, conditional styles can be useful, especially if the document structure is not too complex.

Defining conditional styles

Conditional styles are an answer to those who claim that styles are too difficult to remember. With conditional styles, you only need to remember the name of a single paragraph style per document or template, yet format quickly in different ways.

Admittedly, the available contexts are limited, but they may still be enough for many purposes. You might think of conditional styles as equivalent to single-style outlining – an advanced trick that can be useful and free you from thinking about formatting.

To create a conditional style:

1 Examine a CONDITION tab and make a note of the contexts you want to use. You cannot create new contexts.

2 Create or format a paragraph style for each context you plan to use. The only pre-defined style that you can use as a conditional style is TEXT BODY, but you can create a new style from any pre-defined one.

3 Create a new paragraph style and go to the CONDITION tab. Under OPTIONS, select the CONDITIONAL STYLE box.

Tip

To minimize confusion, name the style CONDITIONAL TEXT or something like SINGLE STYLE so you can identify it.

Otherwise, as you work, you might wonder why the formatting has changed but the style listed on the tool bar hasn't.

4 Highlight a context on the CONDITION tab.

5 In the PARAGRAPH STYLES pane on the CONDITION tab, select the paragraph style that you want to apply in the highlighted context. Click twice, and the selected style is listed under APPLIED STYLES on the right side of the CONTEXT pane.

6 Repeat Step 4–5 as often as needed.

Caution

If you want to use conditions with a custom style, you must set at least one before you close the dialog window. If you do not set at least one condition, the tab will be unavailable the next time you open the style's dialog window.

So long as you have set at least one condition, you can add and delete conditions later.

7   Click the OK or APPLY button when all the contexts you plan to use are associated with a paragraph style.

Setting page breaks by style

The application of a particular paragraph style often coincides with the start of a new page.

For example, new chapters may always start with a paragraph style called CHAPTER NUMBER or TITLE, while a style called DIAGRAM TITLE might begin a new page to ensure plenty of space for a diagram.

This feature is set up in the BREAK section of the TEXT FLOW tab for a paragraph style.

Automating page breaks

To set up automatic page breaks:

1   Open the dialog window for the paragraph style that will coincide with the start of a new page.

2   Select TEXT FLOW tab > BREAKS > INSERT.

3   Set the TYPE to PAGE.

---

4   If the POSITION is BEFORE, you can select the WITH PAGE STYLE box, and choose the new page's style from the drop-down list.

5   When you select a page style to follow the break, you can also re-set the PAGE NUMBER. For example, you might have a page style for an introduction numbered in lower case Roman numerals, and ordinary pages that use Arabic numerals.

6   If you want the page number to continue sequentially from the previous page, leave the PAGE NUMBER field set to o.

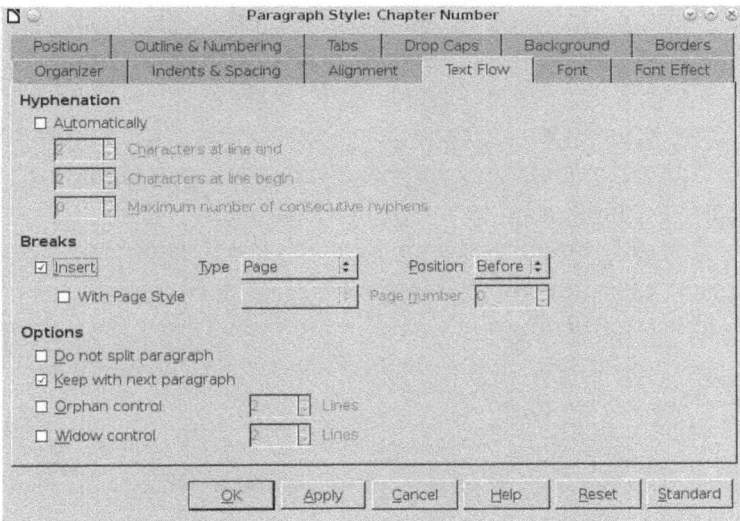

Automate page breaks in the BREAKS section of the TEXT FLOW tab by associating them with a paragraph style. This setting is used mostly to start new chapters in a long document or a master document.

Other common uses include starting a page reserved for an image that occupies an entire page, or inserting a landscape page in an otherwise portrait-oriented document.

STOP

Caution

The TYPE of break also includes the option of COLUMN. This selection may be useful in a multi-column section or a newsletter. However, it can be awkward and confusing. In many cases, you are likely to have less trouble with items shifting if you create a table instead.

Single-sourcing by hiding text

Multiple versions of documents that differ only in some details are common in business or academia. For instance, you might want one version of a handout for students, and another version for teachers that adds teaching goals and suggestions for use. Or, you might have one version of a software manual for users and another for system administrators.

The only trouble is that maintaining multiple versions of a document is difficult. Placing each version in its own file complicates keeping all the versions in sync. Forget just once to update all versions, and correcting the mistake can cost you several painstaking hours.

Yet in most word processors, maintaining all versions in a single file complicates printing, forcing you to create a duplicate copy first, and then to delete all the parts not needed for the version you are printing and hope that you don't make a mistake.

LibreOffice's solution to this dilemma is to create a single file in which selected words, paragraphs, or sections are hidden or revealed as needed. The tools include styles and fields. All the tools for hidden elements work with two versions of the text, but sections and some fields do not work with three or more versions.

Character and Paragraph Styles

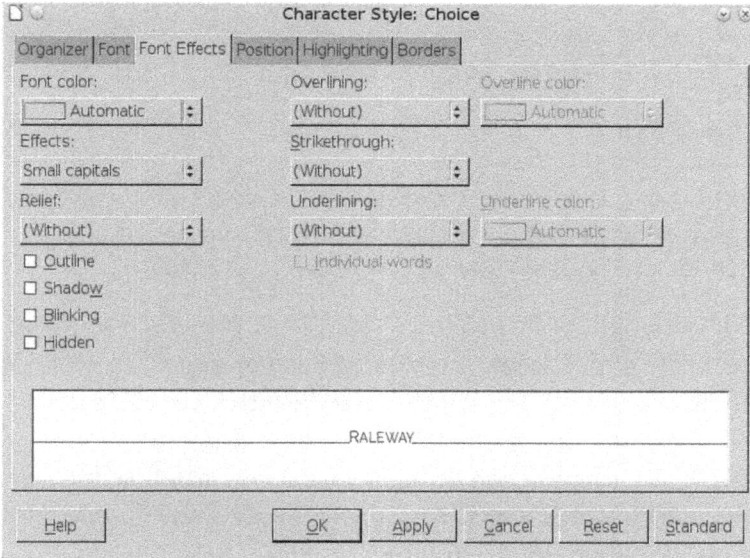

```
┌─────────────────────────────────────────────────────────────┐
│ □ ○              Character Style: Choice              ○ ⊗      │
├─────────────────────────────────────────────────────────────┤
│ Organizer│Font│Font Effects│Position│Highlighting│Borders│    │
│                                                               │
│ Font color:            Overlining:          Overline color:   │
│ [  ] Automatic  [≑]    (Without)     [≑]    [  ] Automatic [≑] │
│ Effects:               Strikethrough:                         │
│ Small capitals  [≑]    (Without)     [≑]                      │
│ Relief:                Underlining:          Underline color: │
│ (Without)       [≑]    (Without)     [≑]    [  ] Automatic [≑] │
│ □ Outline              □ Individual words                     │
│ □ Shadow                                                      │
│ □ Blinking                                                    │
│ □ Hidden                                                      │
│                                                               │
│          ┌──────────────────────────────────────┐            │
│          │              RALEWAY                  │            │
│          └──────────────────────────────────────┘            │
│                                                               │
│ │ Help │        │ OK │ │ Apply │ │ Cancel │ │ Reset │ │ Standard │ │
└─────────────────────────────────────────────────────────────┘
```

Maintaining two copies of the same document in a single file is
as easy as toggling on or off the HIDDEN box at the bottom left of
the FONT EFFECTS tab.

Using hidden text is faster than manual formatting and
reduces the chances of making mistakes. It also eliminates the
need to print from copies, which with careless hands or tired
brains can lead to the accidental over-writing of the original file.

Choosing a tactic for hiding/showing text

Features for hiding and showing text can be used in two ways.

If two versions of the document share common text, enter one
using ordinary paragraph styles and create unique paragraph
styles for the other that can be hidden and shown as needed. This
method works with both styles and with sections and fields, but
can be hard to organize.

User Always On	Admin On/Off	Coders On/Off

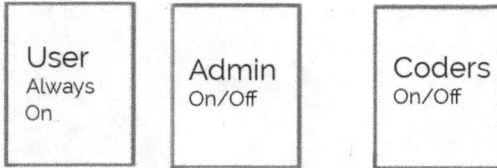

One way to structure single-sourcing is to have one set of styles, sections, or fields that are always visible and another set for each additional version that can be turned on and off.

The alternative is to create a special set of paragraph styles for each version of the document, turning them on and off as needed.

In this structure, each version could be distinct, and single-sourcing mainly a method of keeping related material together. Alternatively, each version could be mixed and matched. For example, if you were preparing user, developer, and admin guides for a piece of software, the published guide for administrators might require showing both the user and admin material, while the guide for developers might include both the admin and developer material. You might also create multiple bodies of content found in more than one version, although that might become too complex to work with. All these possibilities can be used by setting up multiple variables for fields (see "Hiding text using fields," page 92), one for each version, but are least confusing when working with styles only.

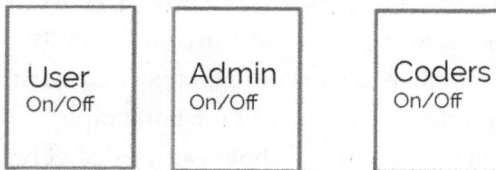

User On/Off	Admin On/Off	Coders On/Off

Another way to single source is to have separate sets of styles, fields, and sections for each version of the document, turning each on and off as needed

No matter how you work, single-sourcing can be confusing, so choose the name of styles and fields to help keep everything straight. You can even give each paragraph style a different font color to make it quickly recognizable. Each style's font color can be replaced quickly by using EDIT > FIND & REPLACE. If you are printing in black and white and use dark enough colors, you may not even need to change the colors when you print.

Hiding text using styles

To hide or reveal text, you can toggle the HIDDEN box on a style's FONT EFFECT tab. You can either choose part of the document to hide to produce one alternative version, or else create a different set of paragraph styles for each version.

Whatever method you choose:

1   Create one set of character and paragraph styles for text that appears in all versions of the document.

2   Create the common styles needed for each version of the text. For example, in a student quiz with an answer key, you might have one set of styles with names like USER – TEXT BODY and TEACHER – TEXT BODY. These styles are formatted exactly the same as the common styles, and hidden as needed.

Tip

You may not need to copy all the common styles for each version of the file. For example, in a quiz, the teacher's version might only need a single paragraph style called ANSWER KEY.

3   On the FONT EFFECT tab, toggle HIDDEN as needed before printing. Notice that spacing above or below a paragraph is

hidden along with the text. By contrast, you need to select the space after a string of hidden characters.

4   After you print a version from a single-source file, de-select HIDDEN so the complete file is visible the next time you open it.

Hiding text using fields

A more time-consuming way of single-sourcing is to place each passage in its own field. Usually, though, this second method is practical only for relatively short documents.

When you single-source, the FUNCTIONS tab of the FIELDS dialog contains several useful tools: HIDDEN TEXT, HIDDEN PARAGRAPH, and CONDITIONAL TEXT. Other types of fields exist, but, except for SET VARIABLE, are not relevant to single-sourcing.

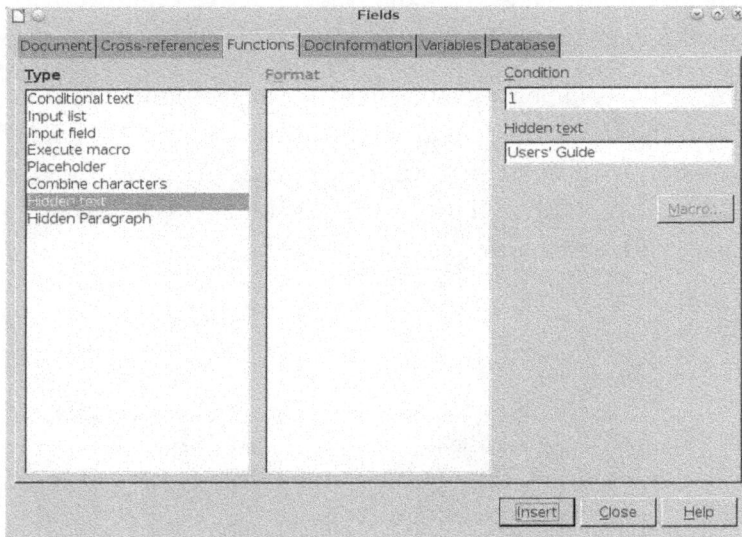

The HIDDEN TEXT field window.

For very limited uses, such as changing the title or the contents of a header or footer, you can use INPUT LISTS, which contains interchangeable items. However, input lists are impractical in a longer document, because each has to be changed separately.

The HIDDEN option in a character or paragraph style is the stylistic equivalent of some of the fields in INSERT > FIELDS > OTHER > FUNCTION > TYPE, such as HIDDEN TEXT and HIDDEN PARAGRAPH.

Caution

Make sure that VIEW > FIELD SHADINGS and VIEW > HIDDEN PARAGRAPHS are turned on when you use these fields. Otherwise, you will be lucky to find the hidden text or paragraphs.

The fields used for single-sourcing use an off or on condition for hiding and unhiding. A condition is merely a state of a document – or, if you prefer, a version with different content.

For instance, when a condition is set to o, then the content in the fields is hidden, creating one version of the file. When a condition is set to 1, then the content is shown, creating a second version. Alternatively, the condition that turns one version of a document on could be the name of the version, such as USER GUIDE. This arrangement is no different than checking or unchecking the HIDDEN box in a style.

Tip

A HIDDEN TEXT field can be awkward, because the field for entering it makes only a limited amount of text visible at one time. Hiding a section may be a simpler tactic to use.

Alternatively, in a CONDITIONAL TEXT field, a simple expression is set up using the CONDITION, THEN, and ELSE fields on the right side of the window. For instance, if the condition is 1, then the text that appears in the document is whatever is entered in the THEN field, such as USER'S GUIDE. However, change the condition to anything else, and the text in the document becomes whatever is entered in the ELSE field, such as SYSTEM ADMINISTRATOR'S GUIDE.

This arrangement is almost as handy as the HIDDEN box in a style. In effect, the CONDITION field becomes a password to limit who can change the condition.

The main disadvantage of this method is that each condition needs to be changed separately, while using the HIDDEN FONT effect means toggling a single box.

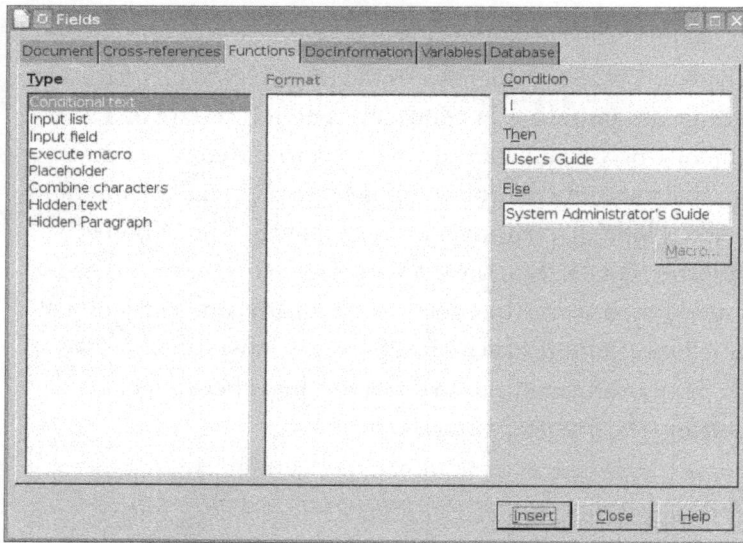

Do not confuse a CONDITIONAL TEXT field with a CONDITIONAL paragraph style. A CONDITIONAL TEXT field is similar to the HIDDEN check box on a paragraph style's FONT EFFECTS tab.

Hiding with sections

When documents have large areas to hide or show, you may prefer using sections. Sections can be used more easily than fields for hiding long passages, but they are less versatile than a paragraph style.

Sections are areas that have properties that are different from the main body of text. These properties may be formatting, or content that is password-protected from editing.

You can also add a link to insert a separate file in the current document. Such links can be another sort of single-sourcing, allowing content used in several documents to be maintained in one place.

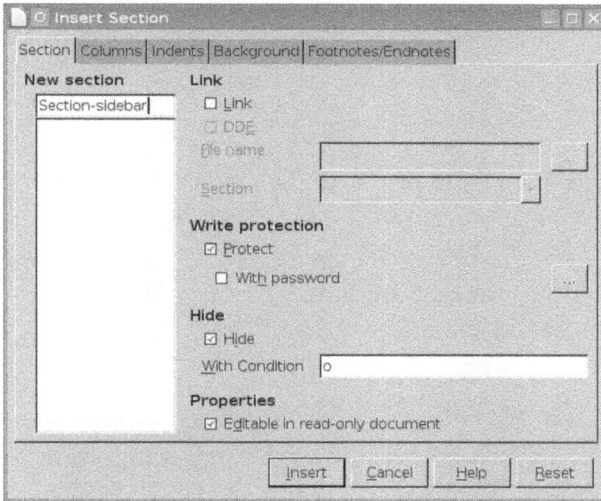

INSERT > SECTION can hide or reveal large sections of text.

Sections work in much the same way as fields:

1 Place the cursor where you want an empty section, or else highlight existing text. Then select INSERT > SECTION. The INSERT SECTION dialog window opens.

2 Give the section a unique name that reflects its contents, and if desired protect it with a password.

3 Click the HIDE box, and/or set the WITH CONDITION field to 1. Either is necessary, but not both. When you close the dialog window, the section and the space above and below it are no longer visible in the document.

Tip

A section set to hide is visible until you remove the mouse cursor from it.

4 When you want to edit the section, click FORMAT > SECTIONS. The dialog window lists the document's sections, with an open or closed lock beside each name to indicate whether it is hidden. Sections can be formatted without unlocking them, but must be unlocked to edit the text.

Automating the use of fields and sections

Field windows stay open after you insert a field, allowing you to move to the next position for a field in the document. Section windows do not, although you can use the Navigator to jump from one section to the next as you edit.

However, changing the conditions for each field or section individually eats up time. If the same field appears more than once, you can copy and paste or use EDIT > AUTOTEXT so that you can add information with a couple of keystrokes, instead of making changes manually.

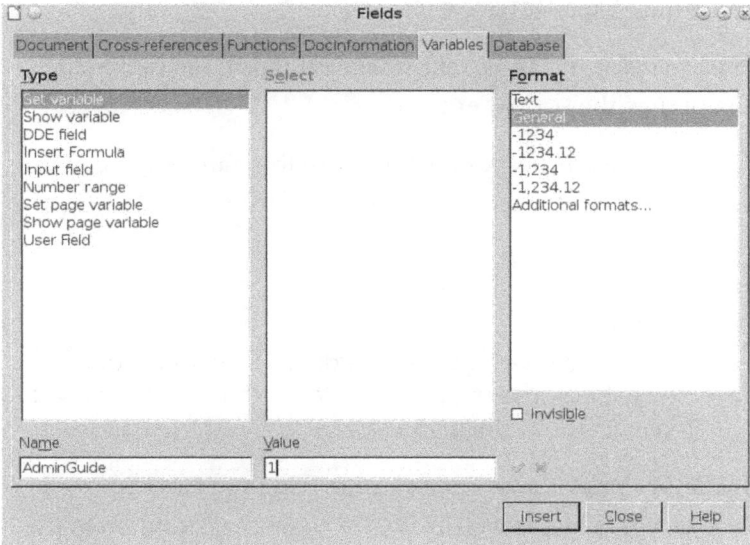

A variable can be a master control for turning all fields with the same condition on or off.

Better yet, you can set a general variable that toggles all fields at the same time:

1   Place the cursor at the start or end of the document, or anywhere else that is easy to locate.

2   Click INSERT > FIELDS > MORE FIELDS > VARIABLES > SET VARIABLE.

3   Set the FORMAT. You can leave it as GENERAL, or specifically as TEXT or a number format.

4 At the bottom of the window, give the variable a name. The name can indicate one of the document versions, or be something like MASTERSWITCH.

5 Enter a value. It can be text, or simply 0 or 1, but make sure that it uses the FORMAT entered.

6 Click the INVISIBLE box so that the variable cannot be seen in the document. Then click the INSERT button.

STOP

Caution

Locating the variable can be difficult, so you should place it in some easy to find place. You might choose to leave it visible while you work.

7 In all the CONDITIONAL TEXT, HIDDEN TEXT, and HIDDEN PARAGRAPH fields, as well as SECTIONS, set the condition to the variable name, followed by the value in quotation marks. For example: MASTERSWITCH "0" or ADMINGUIDE"1".

Condition

MasterSwitch "1"

Hidden text

Programmer's Guide

A HIDDEN TEXT field set up to work with a variable called MASTERSWITCH. The value of the variable follows its name.

Now you can show or hide all the fields in the document by changing only the variable, much as you would with a style.

If you have more than two versions of the document, you can create other variables to toggle each one off and on.

However, make sure that the values are different for each, and that each is placed where you can easily find them. The easiest way to find the values is to use EDIT > TRACK CHANGES > MANAGE CHANGES, especially when the document is complete and the only changes you are marking are hiding or showing different versions.

Automating advanced features

By now, you should understand why Writer can best be described as a desktop publisher. Using Writer, you can follow basic typographic principles and easily design complicated documents.

However, for years, the most advanced typographical features were difficult to use in LibreOffice. Features such as diagonal fractions, small caps, old style figures and ligatures – redrawings of groups of characters to make them easier to read – could sometimes be added by enabling special font files. More often, they could only be added by opening INSERT > SPECIAL CHARACTERS. Installing the Typography Toolbar extension made these features more accessible, but only for the handful of fonts designed to use Graphite, a tool for adding advanced features.

These limitations still apply to versions of LibreOffice before 5.3, and to Apache OpenOffice. However, starting with the 5.3 release, LibreOffice's font-rendering engine automatically uses advanced features for OpenType fonts if the font supports them. For example, instead of using two separate fs, LibreOffice uses the special ligature ff.

If an advanced feature is available in a font file, it will appear in the INSERT > SPECIAL CHARACTER dialog. You can force its automatic use or turn it off in any field to specify a font by typing a code tag written in lower case characters directly after the font name, without any space in-between. For instance, :smcp or :smcp=on will both automatically turn lower case letters into small capitals. If you want to turn off the use of small capitals, add :-smcp or :smcp=off. Multiple snippets can be added one after the other, so that :liga:onum:cpsp forces the use of standard ligatures, old style figures, and kerning for upper case letters, so long as the font supports these features.

In some cases, only the long form can be used because you need to specify a variable. For example, :frac=1 forces the use of smaller-sized fractions with a diagonal separator, while :frac=2 forces the use of smaller-sized fractions with a horizontal separator.

A complete list of available tags, including those for writing systems that do not use Latin characters, is available at: https://en.wikipedia.org/wiki/List_of_typographic_features #OpenType_typographic_features

Family
Fanwood:smcp=1|

Advanced codes can be entered in any field for a font name.

Different font files support different feature sets, so you will have to experiment to learn what you can do with each font. Similarly, the complete list of character codes is likely to have entries whose use is not immediately obvious. However, some of the most useful features are listed in the table below.

Code	Function
:smcp	Converts uppercase letters to small capitals.
:liga	Applies standard ligatures.
:pnum	Converts old style figures to proportional figures.
:onum	Converts all figures to old style figures.
:frac=1	Converts fractions to smaller-sized fractions with a diagonal line.
:frac=2	Converts fractions to small-sized fractions with a horizontal line.
:kern	Kerns characters.

You can ignore these advanced features if you prefer. However, if you want your documents to have the most professional touches available, they are easy to add. Place them in your paragraph and character styles and templates, and you can use them without ever having to think about them again.

Index

horizontal spacing 27
HTML
    document template 65
    styles 61
    tags 63
HTML Tidy 65
hyphenation options 24

I

indentation
    common uses for 27
    first line of paragraph 29
    minimizing 27
    paragraph 27
    quotation 27

K

keep with next paragraph 20
kerning 75

L

languages 58
leading 15
letter template, designing 31
LibreOffice documentation 8
line spacing
    consistent 78
    fixed 14
    proportional 15
    small font sizes 15

vertical 13
lists 50
    nesting 52
    skipping a paragraph 57
    styles 53
locales 58

M

magic number 14
manual formatting 12
maximum number of
consecutive hyphens 25
measurement unit 10
multi-page display 11
multiple languages 58
multiple pages, displaying 11

O

OpenOffice 13, 97
OpenType fonts 97
orphans and widows 18
outlining 50
    paragraph styles 54
    single paragraph style 55

P

page breaks, automating 84
paragraph indentation 27
paragraph numbering,
restarting 52

www.ingramcontent.com/pod-product-compliance
Lightning Source LLC
Chambersburg PA
CBHW031950190326
41519CB00007B/740